PIECES
OF
YOU

ISBN: 978-1-960810-72-4
Pieces of You

Yorkshire Publishing
2488 E 81st St.
Ste 2000
Tulsa, OK 74137
www.YorkshirePublishing.com
918.394.2665

Printed in Canada.

April Farlow

PIECES OF YOU

Knowing Who You Are in Light of Whose You Are

Yorkshire Publishing
TULSA

PIECES

OF

YOU

Contents

Dedication

To the dads in my life:

Dad, you loved me so much that I had to expand my mind to think God could love me more. Through your daily love for me, I have seen glimpses of God's love. By your example, I found the man I wanted to be the father of my children.

My brother, Richard, is my father's living legacy. I'll be forever grateful for your care and concern as you demonstrated to our family that you will "sacrifice for those you love." You demonstrated this in how you cared for Dad and us. I know our dad is smiling down with pride for the father you are today.

My husband, Kip, your love for me and our girls is one of the greatest gifts I have ever experienced. My dad knew you were the one for me. He said you cherished me and that he liked the way you looked at me. And now, you cherish our children in the same way, which is an incredible blessing to witness.

And my Heavenly Father, who loves me most of all.

Introduction

On the day I was born, my dad called his parents from the delivery room to tell them I had arrived. As he waited for the connection, he exclaimed into the phone, "Operator, Operator, it's a girl!"

He picked my name from a song called "Pieces of April" by Three Dog Night. As far as I know, I am the only person named after a song by a band that sings about a bullfrog named Jeremiah. As I grew up, Dad created secret nicknames just for me, adding new names to increase my anticipation for what he'd call me next.

Over time, one name stuck:

Lydia April Snodgrass Jabaroni Gertrude Mahoney Whirley.

Silly to most, but to me, the sweetest name in the world.

Dad taught me to build campfires, negotiate business deals, and dream about who I wanted to become. He gave me permission to ask hard questions and explore my beliefs. He taught me how a man should treat me by demonstrating his love for my mom. We talked a lot about God together, too. He let me explore my faith, all the while showing his faith in me in the way he lived and loved.

As a teenager, my dad used the long commute to school to help me navigate the tough questions in life. Little did I know these moments had the potential to shape my identity for better or worse. Every time I got out of the car, Dad said the same thing to close the conversation and send me out into my day:

"Remember who you are, and remember I love you."

With that one simple sentence, my dad helped shape the pieces of who I am by reminding me constantly of Whose I am.

Over time, those words made an impact on how I came to see myself, but also on how I came to see God. I never had to question how much a God in Heaven could love me because my dad loved me so well on Earth. But I had difficulty imagining anyone could love me as much as my dad! Unashamedly, I am a daddy's girl. That's a badge of honor I have worn proudly my entire life. I thought it was the highest compliment anyone could give me: to reflect the man I admired most.

Because of him, I know who I am, but more importantly, I know *Whose* I am.

But, of course, this sense of self didn't come without a fight. One would think with the kind of love and guidance my dad gave me, I'd be able to walk through life with an unshakeable assurance in my identity.

Well, that assumption would be wrong.

On the outside, it looked like I had it all together. As an adult, I passed my days teaching Dale Carnegie classes with titles like "How to Win Friends and Influence People" and "How to Stop Worrying and Start Living." But on the inside? Well, I was barely staying afloat.

"Fake it until you make it."

That was another motto Dad instilled in me. I was leading other people but silently struggling to lead myself. The pieces of me I presented to the world were the shiny, bright, successful pieces I wanted others to see. But the pieces I was dealing with on the inside were the messy, broken, hurt pieces nobody knew about. If I'm honest, it remained that way for years. I kept faking it until I couldn't make it anymore.

Then, I finally got it together.

Fast forward a decade, and the pieces of my life the world sees still look very much the same. I still teach classes. I still guide and encourage executives in the corporate space. And miraculously, people still think I am capable of doing so. However, those other pieces of me—the hidden pieces—have completely transformed. Now, I do have some important things in my life figured out, and they might not be perfect, but I feel good about them.

I feel confident in what has been repaired.

The truth is that the reparation happened to me in an honest, raw, and unexpected way. And once I was in it, I was left with a choice: Stay here or grow.

I am so thankful I chose the latter.

Take caution here and brace for impact. Because throughout this jour-ney, there have been rock-bottom times. Ugly-cry times. Completely and utterly gross, I-don't-want-to-tell-you-about times. Yet it's these times that others might understand the most. It's these times that make my repair worth the share. Because, if we're honest, won't we all eventually find ourselves in need of a little repair?

Recently, I have worked with kids who are aging out of foster care, and it has given me a chance to walk in real-time with young adults preparing to launch into adulthood. It has solidified, for me, the importance of addressing every piece of who I am and Whose I am. It even prompted me to start a non-profit called Lydia's Place, where we serve and house young adults who have faced homelessness or foster care. During their stay at Lydia's Place, students meet for group ses-sions to discuss their struggles and sort through their hard questions about life. Many of the young adults who come to Lydia's Place never had parental support, and most never experienced the love and guid-ance of a father. They're struggling to figure out who they are without any understanding of how loved they are—without any understand-ing of *Whose* they are. Through no fault of their own, they've got some repairs to navigate, too.

Over the last twenty years, I have spent more days than I can count helping and coaching my students. During these coaching sessions, we have worked on figuring out the pieces of who they are so they can cast bigger visions for their future. But throughout the years, I have been unable to share the most significant piece of life's puzzle: God's love. Understandably, I'm not permitted to talk about faith in most corporate settings, and it has made my job tricky at times because, as I have repeatedly discovered, it is hard to help students figure out who they are when I cannot talk about Whose they are. Even if the business leaders don't realize it, that's ultimately what we're talking about. They're working through some repairs of their own, too.

I'm a mother now. And because of that, my life is filled with other women who are also navigating the tricky path of motherhood. We're all trying to figure out how to raise our children in a healthy, helpful way. To point them to a God who loves them and wants to guide them. To help them get to the other side of childhood with security in who they are and Whose they are. Of course, repairs are being worked out regularly in motherhood, too.

For the coworkers in your office,
The people sitting in the pew with you at church,
The family members around your table at the holidays,
The partner you've chosen in marriage or dating,
The friends you rely on ...

There are always repairs to be made. There are broken, scattered pieces that need to be rearranged and new pieces that need to be put together.

And, as it turns out, regardless of what pieces of your life you're working through, the questions you begin asking as you process are typically the same.

Who am I?
How do I navigate the relationships in my life?
What do I believe?
What are the rules?
What is important?
Do I matter?
Where do I want to go?

This sameness in our search—these questions everyone asks as they work to become the people they're made to be—is the force driving me to write. Because they're all questions I've asked myself. They're truths I've grappled with in my struggle to repair. They're all things I've considered in putting my own pieces together. And in my journey to answer them, I've discovered something invaluable along the way—something I want to share to help others discover for themselves, too.

It's there in the words my father shared every day of my childhood:

"Remember who you are, and remember I love you."

To repair, to grow, to change, to fully be the people God has made you to be, you must start with these pieces. You must know assuredly not just who you are, but Whose you are. You must clearly define it so that you can fully embrace it. You must put those pieces together.

That's what I hope to do in the pages of this book.

A word of warning before you go on. Fully embracing who you are is hard. If it could be done in a two-hour seminar, I'd be a millionaire! The reality is it's messy. It hurts. It's often lonely. Yet, I hope you'll trust me when I tell you it's also beautiful. Going through this journey, I didn't just bandage what was broken and try to move on. Instead, I took a long look in the mirror, did some hard internal work, and changed from the inside out. The reflection I see looking back at me now? A woman who feels confident in every piece of who she is. A woman who is sure not just in who I am but, more importantly, in Whose I am.

Being able to rest securely in those two truths is what I believe my father wanted for me. And it's what I want for others, too. To find the answers to the most profound questions you're asking. To fully embrace every piece of who you are. To rest securely in the truth that you belong to a loving God.

This story would have been easier to write if it were all in hindsight. The reality is that I started writing about a season of repair in my early twenties, yet here I am today, walking through another one all over again.

When I was one year into writing this book, a book so deeply inspired by the words of my father, he passed away. To say this loss shattered me beyond words is an understatement. The grief is real and raw, and the need for a new kind of repair in my life is overwhelming. All over again, I am discovering who I am without the man I have always looked to as a compass.

Along the way, I figured out that I had to lean on my Heavenly Father to connect with my earthly father. And it was in that space that I discovered the greatest compliment of all: to be a daddy's girl, though not the way I always thought it to be true. Yes, I am the daughter of Rick Whirley, and I know without a doubt that for the entirety of his life, I was loved by him. Because of him, I knew who I was and Whose I was. But in this new world—this world without him in it physically—I know that I am the daughter of a Heavenly Father. I am who I am because of the God who made me, shaped my identity, and loves me unconditionally.

In Him, I know without a doubt who I am and Whose I am.

Once I centered my life around Whose I am, understanding who I am got really simple. The repairs felt manageable. The pieces came together. My values, beliefs, rules, relationships, and even my purpose—all the answers to the big questions I was asking—became more apparent when I focused the lens of my identity on Him.

Even without my dad here to remind me, I still know who I am and Whose I am. They've become the most significant pieces—the foundational truths—that I lean on and return to in my repairs even now.

I want to help you discover the same important foundational truths for yourself. I want to guide you in putting together the pieces of your life so that you can fully become who you are as you rest in Whose you are.

Along the way, I pray that you will discover the intimate, personal love of a Father who loves you immeasurably more than you can imagine. That you would come to believe you can do more than you have imagined when God is at work in you. That every piece of your life would be rooted in His love.

So, are you willing? Are you ready to take that look in the mirror? To put your pieces together?

Together, let's discover the truth of who you are and Whose you are.

Together, let's look at the pieces of you.

CHAPTER ONE
The Compared Piece

My mother is a collector.

Our family has had rental properties since I was an infant, so the collections range from furniture and sentimental items left by tenants to items found on sale that might help stage a home. My mom loves to share about a deal that she found or to use something she saved for the perfect occasion. And while she may be proud of everything she's collected over the years, my favorite is her collection of kaleidoscopes.

Throughout my childhood, my mom collected kaleidoscopes to display inside her glass-top coffee table. It made for a great conversation about the thoughtful gifts people shared with her or the places she'd visited. To this day, Mom still remembers in detail where she got each kaleidoscope, the person who gave it to her, and the occasion it was gifted to her. There is a memory for each one in the collection.

As an adult, I realized I am a collector in my own right (Like mother, like daughter, right?). My most prized collection, however, is not of kaleidoscopes but of people.

See, some people have a core group of friends. Maybe they have high school friends they grew up with and carried into adulthood. Perhaps they met in college, taking on some of life's biggest changes and challenges together along the way. Maybe they're friends made at church, in the school pickup line, at a party, or at work.

However you found them, they're your people. The ones you call for quick texts and long talks. The ones you take on lunch dates and weekend trips. The ones you show up for, without a doubt. The ones who show up when the chips are down. The ones who celebrate the major moments in life.

I always thought it would be special to have a tight group of friends who have a running text thread. What I have is not that. It's a random collection of incredible people who don't all know each other, still, they support me, love me, fight for me, and show up for me. They're steadfast friends willing to tell me the truth in any situation. They ground me, surround me, and generally astound me with their ability to be honest, loving, incredible friends.

They are my Kaleidoscopes.

In preparation for writing this book, I invited thirty women to come together and help brainstorm some of the content. If I want someone to tell me the truth, I will get it from my Kaleidoscopes.

In putting this group together, I didn't just ask the friends who were closest to me. I tried to piece together a group of women from different areas of life, different perspectives, and different backgrounds. After all, aren't our differences what make us unique? Aren't those details what make each view in a kaleidoscope distinct?

I asked each woman to answer some in-depth questions the day we gathered.

Asking these ladies to look honestly at the pieces of who they are and share about themselves with women they didn't necessarily know was an intense way to begin, but from their vulnerability came so much beauty.

For starters, I asked some questions about how they see themselves.

When you get quiet and hear your internal voice, what does it say? How would you describe yourself based on that voice?

Take a moment to answer these questions. I hope you'll be willing to get honest with yourself like my Kaleidoscopes did that day. The honesty in their answers stunned me.

High strung	*Clingy*	*Church mouse*
Unorganized	*Critical*	*Busy*
Complicated	*Consistently inconsistent*	*Lack of self-control*
Prissy	*Lazy*	*Impulsive*
Rule follower	*Codependent*	*Wounded*
Unworthy	*Has to be perfect*	*Insignificant*
Impatient	*Weird*	*Angry*
Introverted	*Intimidating*	*Alone*
Infertile	*Divorced*	*Bad mom*
Workaholic	*Unappreciated*	*Sad*

This list doesn't even begin to scratch the surface. I could have created an entirely separate category for just the "too" phrases on the lists.

Too churchy

Too uptight

Too sensitive

Too opinionated

Too laid back

Too needy

Too emotional

Too big

Too much

Too independent

Too emotional

Too old to have young kids

Too high maintenance

Too much debt

Too small

Then, there was the lengthy list of "not" statements.

Not working

Not religious enough

Not healthy

Not pretty enough

Not in a relationship

Not a good friend

Not good enough to make a friend

Not enough money

Not serious

Not balanced

Not successful

Not educated

Not a professional

Not as much fun as I used to be

Not a mom

That's a doozy of a list, isn't it?

On the drive home that day, I rode in silence to unpack the impact of the gathering. What made this first meeting of my Kaleidoscopes so powerful, not just for me but for them as well?

Had this group been friends on social media, they may have recognized each other, but only known each other by their highlight reels. Highlights of family vacations, perfectly prepared meals, and orchestrated snapshots that make our lives look as close to Hallmark as possible. Highlight reels that make it almost impossible not to fall into the comparison trap.

Had they known each other closely, they might've felt tempted to hold back their answers. They might've been afraid to speak up for fear of being compared. For fear of not measuring up to the rest of the women in the room. For fear that the pieces of who they are wouldn't be enough.

Perhaps this was the reason this moment was so special. These women came in with their guards down. They were ready, willing, and able to be honest with me and one another because they came in without context to compare. Maybe that's what gave them the courage to share about ...

The hard marriages,
The miscarriages,
The lost jobs,
The cancer and hard medical diagnoses,
The deaths of children, spouses, parents,
The destroyed hopes or dreams,
The abuse,
The trauma,
The financial disasters,
The affairs,
The failed friendships,
The struggles around body image and weight,
The mom guilt.

The more they shared, the more they found in common. Over just a few hours, my Kaleidoscopes began to lean into each other's stories. Things got real fast. And I think that's because we took a break from measuring ourselves against each other. Instead of comparing, we chose to share.

And that's a great place to start.

To stand confidently in both who you are and Whose you are, you must first learn to avoid the temptation to compare. Staying out of the comparison trap is an essential piece of the puzzle that is discovering and embracing our identity.

After our meeting, my friend Angela went home and looked in her daughter's school folder. There, she found a worksheet her seven-year-old, Elle, had filled out. "Color yourself and then write words to describe yourself in the circles," the instructions said across the top. That's precisely what Elle did. She colored her hair and eyes to match hers and wrote six words to describe herself.

Funny
Artistic
Pretty
Love
Kind
Smart

For Angela, her daughter's list was not only accurate, but it was also a stark contrast to the list she and the other women had made. Angela told me about it later: "I wonder at what age we stop believing the good? I wonder what happens to cause us to begin seeing the negative before the positive?"

I wonder the same for all of us.

What experiences have shaped the way you see yourself?
What is it that you believe about who you really are?
Where did the idea of who you're supposed to be come from?

How does trying to measure up make you feel?

The fact is, we're conditioned to compare every piece of ourselves from the beginning. When babies are born, they're announced with their height, weight, and general markers for their health. As they grow up, those stats are measured against others.

Your child is in the 90th percentile for height.
Your baby is in the 5th percentile for weight.
Your kid is not developmentally appropriate compared to others their age.

While I don't remember baby growth charts, I remember the chart hanging in my kindergarten class. The giant giraffe hanging on the wall tormented me each month as our teacher would have us stand against the wall to measure our growth. I dreaded the day each time it came around because I knew I would always fall short … literally. I was so short that I didn't even reach the neck, so the teacher had to mark my height on the giraffe's body. I was the only one who couldn't seem to get up to that stupid giraffe's neck, and you better believe I noticed.

In my mind, I quite literally didn't measure up in comparison to everyone else.

Now, as the mom of young kids, I often hear the funny ways children compare themselves to each other without realizing that's what they're doing.

How many years are you?
How many teeth have you lost?
How many sight words can you read?
How many dolls do you have?

How many jumps can you do?

Of course, as we grow up, those points of comparison change.

How many points did you score?
What degree did you get?
How many followers do you have?
What grade did you get on that test?
How much money do you make?

Are they prettier than me? Smarter than me? Have more friends than me?

Why are they married, but I'm not?
Why is their house so much nicer?
Why is their child potty trained already?
Why are their children successful while mine are flailing?
Why do they have the grandchildren I want so badly?
What makes their life seem so much better than mine?

No wonder so many people are exhausted! We've been fighting our way out of the comparison trap since birth, and somehow, we aren't any closer to winning. That's because measuring up is a constant, winless cycle. When we compare ourselves to others, it causes us to overlook the good in our lives for the sake of looking at what seems better in someone else's. It forces our eyes away from what's true about who we are and Whose we are and puts them instead on what we believe could be better. It steals our joy and leads to discontentment in almost every area of our lives. It keeps us looking at the pieces of ourselves in frustration and disgust rather than in gratitude and peace.

So, why are we letting comparison continue to be our compass?

There's a ten-year age gap between Lauren, my stepdaughter (or as I say, my bonus daughter), and our younger girls. I remember how often I would drop her off and look around at her friends' homes. Every single time, I let the pieces of their lives make me feel bad about the pieces of my life. How could these people have it all together? They had clean, calm homes, while mine felt like it was burning around me. The chaos I saw in my own life felt magnified every time I dropped Lauren off at one of their homes.

Of course, I never considered these parents were well out of the baby stage. They were no longer dealing with toddlers, plastic toys, and diapers. Looking back, I can see the moments I missed while wondering how they had it together, and I didn't. Now I can see we weren't even playing in the same ballpark. But at the time, I was so wrapped up in comparison and how I failed that I couldn't see the truth that seems so clear to me now.

Comparison breeds rotten fruit. It shapes your identity in a way that only tells us the bad, the negative, the failure. It kills your joy and your confidence. And truth be told, once these beliefs about who you are have taken root, they're hard to remove. Flipping your internal script isn't a quick and easy task.

But if you want to be confidently established in who you are, it's a task you must be willing to take on. Because in every piece of life, you'll find opportunities to compare, to measure up, to question your worth. If you want to stand confidently in who you are, you must turn down the volume on comparison and turn up the volume on something more valuable: The truth of who God is and who He made you to be. You must be willing to do the hard work of uprooting your false beliefs about who you are so that you can make room for God's truth. You must stop the comparison by taking your eyes off others to see who you truly are.

God did not call you to be identical to everyone else. Just like my mom's collection of kaleidoscopes, no two people were made identical. Even if two kaleidoscopes were made with the same parts in the same factory, slight variations would exist. The creator intended for variation in the glass pieces, just as our Creator intended for our pieces to be unique. No two people, no two lives, will be exactly the same.

How do I know? Well, in the words of an old childhood church tune, the Bible tells me so. You may have heard the familiar words of Psalm 139. So often, I see this passage hung on the walls of nurseries or prayed over children in the womb. Let me remind you that these words are true of you no matter your age, phase, or season.

"For you created my inmost being; you knit me together in my mother's womb. I praise you because I am fearfully and wonderfully made" (Psalm 139:13-14a NIV).

To free yourself from the comparison trap, you must focus on who God says you are above all else. You must believe God designed you to be uniquely and wonderfully who you are. Every piece of me and every piece of you? It's exactly how God intended it to be, which should give us both a sense of relief. No piece of you should make me question any piece of me.

My girls love to paint pictures, and I love to display their artwork. Their pieces won't end up in any galleries, but I think they're beautiful. I love their pictures, not because of the colors used, the creativity displayed, or the skills shown, but because of who painted them.

And my girls know that. They aren't worried about what anyone else thinks about their artwork but their father and I, the ones who made them and love them for who they are. They know we love it because they know we love them; it's as simple as that.

I think there's a lesson for you here. What if you could begin to shift your thinking about yourself in the same way? What if you could see your value isn't in what you do, what you accomplish, what you have, or how you look? What if you shape your identity by listening to the One who made you? What if you focused instead on Whose you are as a source of celebrating the pieces of who you are?

I believe you can. And more than that, if you want to stand confidently in your identity, I believe you must.

So, how do you do that? Well, there are a few places I think you can begin.

1. Focus on Whose you are.

The quickest way to turn off comparison is to turn your eyes to the One who made you, to go back to Whose you are. Let the truth you find there remind you who you are and, more importantly, who He is. Your confidence should not come from who you are and what you can accomplish but from who He is and what He can do. He created, crafted, and designed you. He made you because He loves you. You are beautiful and beloved in His eyes, and, most of all, God isn't comparing you to anyone else.

Easier to say than believe, right? Well, when I'm struggling to focus on the truth of who I am because of Whose I am, I go back to the source. Maybe this list of truths about who God says you are will help you the way it helps me.

A child of God -John 1:12
Chosen -John 15:16
Precious -Isaiah 43:4
Unique -Psalm 139:13
Treasured -Deuteronomy 14:2
Important -1 Peter 2:9
Empowered -Philippians 4:13
Protected -Psalm 121:3

2. Pay attention to when you are tempted to compare.

Pay attention to when your thoughts, choices, and words begin the spiral toward the comparison trap. Are you feeling stressed, anxious, or brought down by being around certain people? Or while scrolling through social media? Or while watching TV? Are there places, social settings, or groups of people that push you to become critical of yourself? Where are you overly critical of yourself in general? Do you feel like you're ruminating on other people's milestones, ideas, and achievements rather than celebrating your own? Are you rushing through your life in order not to fall behind? Are you judging others harshly to feel better about yourself? These are signs you may be stuck in a comparison trap.

My husband, Kip, and I joined a small group right after we got married. When we arrived at the first group meeting, we noticed another differentiator between us and the other couples: We were the only blended family. At the time, Lauren was only with us a few nights a week while these families had their children with them every day.

That night, the dinner conversation centered around the activities of their children. I felt like a fish out of water because our circumstances weren't the same. I felt surrounded by people with the family dynamic I wanted but didn't have. Truth be told, it made me feel awful.

Tears began streaming down my face the moment we left. Looking back now, I recognize what was happening. Through my own fault, I let myself get pulled into a comparison trap, which ruined my group experience.

Many of the pieces we are given are beyond our control, yet they are exactly what God is using in our lives to point toward Him. You are looking inward when you feel challenged by comparison when you should look upward toward the God who loves you uniquely.

3. Row your own boat.

As a child, my dad sang, "Row, row, row your boat, gently down the stream." Of course, we had fun as we sang, but he always added a lesson with the tune. He would say, "April, get so focused on rowing your own boat that you don't have time to look at anyone else's." Then he would add, "When you are gentle on yourself, you will float merrily down the stream."

Imagine the freedom to focus on rowing your boat rather than spending so much time watching the boats row by. Instead of giving so much attention to the lives of others, what if you focused on the life God gave you?

When we had been married for a year, Kip and I decided to start trying for a baby. After nearly two years of trying with no success,

I felt inadequate. I adore and love my stepdaughter so much, and it was hard to end our weekends together when she went home to her mom. I craved so much to be fully present to my child, and while I understood the necessity for her to go home, seeing her leave still broke my heart a little more during that specific season.

To make matters worse, many of my friends started having babies. I was attending all the showers, scrolling social media to see all the adorable announcements, and seeing all the cute newborn photos on display. While I was thrilled for my friends, it was all a painful reminder to me and reinforced by beliefs of failure. Their boats seemed filled with babies, while things were decidedly less baby-filled on my side of the stream.

I remember crying to my mom, telling her how I feared I would never experience the family everyone else seemed to have and the one I wanted. Mom, always my voice of reason, gave me some very blunt advice: "April, let's be careful. You are measuring who you are against your friend's uterus. Let's keep that in perspective. This is not who you are; it is just a piece of your story."

She was right, of course.

Later, I had a counselor say it differently: "Be careful judging your insides by other people's outsides." Isn't that true? It is so easy to drive through a neighborhood and make assumptions about the perfect lives everyone else lives based only on the pieces of their lives we can see. Wouldn't we all be more at peace if we stopped looking at their pieces and kept our eyes on our own?

That subtle shift in perspective helped me get through the difficult season. When I became pregnant and had my baby girl, I was grateful, not just for her life, but for the lesson about comparison she unknowingly taught me. She was my reminder to row my own boat.

4. Watch your words and change your narrative.

Sometimes, the only person who knows you're struggling with comparison is you. That's because it starts in your mind. It can be easy to play a narrative about who you are that's fueled by who you aren't. So, you must work to change that narrative. To capture your thoughts and shift them to something else, something better, something true.

Instead of saying, "I am damaged, I am broken, and I have trust issues,"
say, "I am healing, I am discovering myself, and I am learning to trust again."

Instead of saying, "I failed,"
say, "I tried, and I'm learning."

Instead of saying, "I am too much" or "I am not enough,"
say, "I am exactly who God made me to be."

If you're struggling with where to start, call for help. When my Kaleidoscopes were all gathered in the same room that day, I asked another question:

What words would you use to describe your five closest friends?

The list they came up with in response was beautiful.

Beautiful   *Strong*   *Determined*
Loyal   *Good friend*   *Big heart*

31

Thoughtful	*Connector*	*Intelligent*
Encouraging	*Powerful*	*Smart*
Tenderhearted	*Positive*	*Authentic*
Confident	*Good mom*	*Respectful*
Dynamic	*Intentional*	*Dependable*
Compassionate	*Intelligent*	*Giving*
Purposeful	*Patient*	*Devoted*
Kind	*Leader*	*Fun*

Imagine if you let this be the narrative that played in your mind. The good news is you have the power to choose. If you have a hard time with this, consider asking yourself, "What would I speak over my friend in the same situation?" I bet you would extend them more grace, more affirmation than you share with yourself, so try taking your 'own advice.'

When you struggle with negative thoughts, ask God to speak truth to you to help where you need his grace and love to cover your own insecurities. You always have the choice to reframe your words and shift your narrative. And what's more, you have a God who offers to help take those negative thoughts and false beliefs captive, holding them so you don't have to carry them anymore. What a gift to know you don't have to do it on your own.

5. Remember, there's always more to the story.

How often have you observed someone at a distance and believed they had it easy, only to learn they were silently struggling? You can craft what might look like a life put together through the things you post, the clothes you wear, and even the things you say. Be careful to remember that salt and sugar look the same. You don't see the heartache that may hide behind those posts. You don't see the person falling apart beneath the curated outfit and perfect makeup. You don't hear the cries hidden behind smiles and jokes. Remember there's more real to the highlight reel that's not shown.

You can see the car they drive, the house they live in, or the name-brand clothes their kids wear, but there is always more to the story. You can't see the hurtful things they heard as a child, the doubts they experience when they look in the mirror, the horrible thing their teenager said on the way out the door this morning, the dreams that were dashed years ago, the financial struggle that happens behind closed doors each month, the medical diagnosis they can't even talk about yet, or the painful conversation they just had with their spouse. You may not always see the rest of the story, but you have to remember there is always more. Because remembering what you can't see is imperative to helping you shift away from comparison.

Growing up, a friend of mine was often compared to her sister. Close in age and the only two girls in the family, it was easy for others to hold the two of them up to one another. My friend was constantly told, "Oh, you're the smart one, and your sister is the pretty one." Of course, my friend took those words hard. Over time, they eventually drove a wedge between her and her sister. She wanted to be "the pretty one," and watching her sister go on dates, get so much attention, and seem to thrive under that label made it worse.

Eventually, as adults, the two sisters finally shared a conversation about those childhood words. When my friend told her sister how much she wished to be seen as "the pretty one," her sister was shocked.

"I hated that label," she confessed. "It might've looked like I embraced it, but I hated it. I mean, do you know how much I wanted to be seen as smart? As fun? As kind? As anything other than my appearance?

It is hard to believe that the only thing you have going for yourself is that you are pretty."

There's always more to the story. I am always deciphering information through what I think other people think of me, and I am often wrong. Remembering that helped my friend have compassion for herself and her sister, too.

So, as you go forward picking up the pieces of who you are and Whose you are, my first call to you is this: Stop looking beside you. You must be willing to let go of the comparisons between yourself and others. You must row your own boat because it is the one God assigned only for you. When you do, you'll find the freedom to go forward with more confidence in who you are because you know without a doubt that the truth of Whose you are holds you up.

May you heed the words of the Apostle Paul:

"Each one should test their own actions. Then they can take pride in themselves alone, without comparing themselves to someone else, for each one should carry their own load." (Galatians 6:4-5 NIV).

May you know who you are and Whose you are without comparison.

Who You Are

- When you get quiet and hear your inner voice, how would you describe yourself? Do you tend to go positive or negative? Are there words that hurt?
- How would your close friends describe you? How is that different from how you might describe yourself?

- What is your most challenging comparison trap? Something that makes you look longingly at someone else.
- What do you struggle to love about yourself? What can you do to love that part of yourself?

Whose You Are

- Why is it important to consider how you see yourself? Is it to make you feel better about yourself? Or is it to take your eyes off yourself and put them on the truth of God instead?
- What stands out to you about who God says you are? Can you believe this is true for you?
- What makes believing who God says you are difficult?

A Prayer

Dear God,

Thank You for creating me uniquely just as You wanted me to be. Thank You for loving me just as I am. Thank You for not measuring Your love for me against others.

God, it is hard not to compare myself with others. Forgive my jealousy, my envy, and my insecurity. Take my eyes off other people or other circumstances and fix my gaze on You.

Help me look through the lens of Your love and be grateful for how You created me. I pray You are shaping me to be who I am meant to be. Mold me into who You want me to be and help me reflect Your love to the world.

Take all my pieces and use them to point others to You.

Amen.

A Truth to Remember

Therefore, since we are surrounded by such a great cloud of witnesses, let us throw off everything that hinders and the sin that so easily entangles. And let us run with perseverance the race marked out for us, fixing our eyes on Jesus, the pioneer and perfecter of faith (Hebrews 12:1-2a NIV).

CHAPTER TWO
The Distorted Piece

During my sophomore year of college, I started dating Mike. He was cute, a baseball player, and intelligent. We dated for a few months, but eventually, I realized a problem: He wasn't into me. I think he liked me well enough, but it was pretty evident that he liked baseball and his friends more.

If my friends thought I was a daddy's girl during middle school and high school, they should have seen me during college. My dad's office was in the same town as my college, and we set boundaries to protect my independence. We agreed never to show up unannounced. But I drove directly to see my dad the day I broke things off with Mike.

This was a boundary-busting day.

However, I immediately regretted busting into his office when I found my dad and all of his employees in the middle of an intense conversation in the boardroom. But when my dad looked up and saw my tears, his entire demeanor changed.

"The meeting is over," he declared without pause.

I held back most of my tears as his employees filed out of the room. When we were left alone, my dad lovingly stood up, hugged me, and said, "Let's go get ice cream."

Ice cream was our secret love language. After all, everything is better when you have ice cream, right? We got to Dairy Queen, ordered our favorite treats, and sat in a booth. As we ate quietly, my dad finally asked, "Are you going to tell me what's going on?"

The dam on my tears burst. It took me a minute to mutter the words, "I broke up with Mike."

Dad paused, looking perplexed. Raising an eyebrow, he said, "Let me get this straight. *You* broke up with *him*? Why are you crying?"

Two hours later, Dad patched me up, dried my tears, and even got me to laugh a bit. Feeling stronger, I returned to school. None of my friends even knew I went to see my dad that day. They didn't know I'd busted up a meeting just to get his help. But when you have the kind of dad who will cancel a meeting and take you to ice cream, you can't help but need him every once in a while.

Oh, there have been so many days since he passed that I have longed for a "Dad fix." Even now, I wish I could call him up for an ice cream visit. I'm comforted to remember how blessed I am to have even had this kind of love from my father. I know this is not the experience all daughters have with their fathers.

When I asked my Kaleidoscopes to describe their relationships with their fathers, I expected them to say, "It was great," or "It was bad," or even "It was just kind of average." But that's not what happened. They came ready to share the details—the good, the bad, and the ugly. Only a third of the women described a relationship like my own. The others had much different experiences with their earthly fathers.

"My dad died when I was four, so I didn't really know what it was like to have a dad in the picture."

"My dad had an affair, and it was the town's embarrassment."

"My dad was focused on his work; he thought providing for our family was the way to love us. He provided for us but wasn't around very much."

"My dad was in and out of jail my whole childhood. I worked hard to follow all the rules so people didn't associate me with him."

"My dad was everyone's friend. He didn't give me a lot of rules or advice; he was more like a friend."

In that small group, there were some tough stories. One shared that she was in a legal battle with her dad even as we were meeting. Others shared about becoming caretakers for their fathers and the change that brought to the relationship. Some shared about seeing their dads grow and age and how it made them aware of how they were blessed to have such a strong, loving dad growing up.

See what I mean? Of all the pieces that make up your life, the relationship you have with your father is a crucial and complicated one. While I know all relationships are important, I truly believe, as a woman, no relationship impacts my understanding of my identity and God Himself more than the one I have with my earthly father. Yes, your earthly father has an incredible impact on your understanding of who you are and Whose you are. He is a huge piece in the puzzle of your identity.

By design, the relationship with your biological dad should prepare you for a relationship with your Heavenly Father. A father's nature provides a window or lens through which you can experience the heart of God. How confusing this must be if the nature of your relationship with a father figure is complex or even just lukewarm. How hard it must be to compare that relationship with a perfect Heavenly Father because it means you must recognize that even the greatest dads aren't perfect.

You see, no matter what kind of relationship you have with your earthly father, he's still distorted pieces at the end of the day. He can never accurately reflect your relationship with your perfect Heavenly Father, and that can make your relationships with both fathers a little harder to understand.

My friend Angie from Lydia's Place grew up in poverty. She wanted so much to have a different future than she had experienced as a child. Angie had no father figure in her life. When she turned eighteen, her mother told her it was time to contribute back to the family. As her mother meant it, Angie needed to get pregnant so that she could collect welfare. Angie had a different vision for her life. She wanted to attend college, get an education, and healthily contribute to her future. So, that's what she decided to do. But with that decision, her family packed her up and sent her out into the world alone.

After meeting us, Angie visited church with our family. She had grown up attending church, though she quickly pointed out that she never felt like she belonged. Knowing the details of her story, I wanted to help. Perhaps she could come to understand God as a Father who could provide the sort of love that her earthly father could not extend.

One Sunday, I noticed Angie weeping beside me quietly as the congregation sang the words from the song "Good, Good Father" by Chris Tomlin.

"Oh, I've heard a thousand stories of what they think You're like
But I've heard the tender whisper of love in the dead of night
And You tell me that You're pleased and that I'm never alone

You're a good, good Father
It's who You are, it's who You are, it's who You are
And I'm loved by You
It's who I am, it's who I am, it's who I am."

I couldn't help but wonder how confusing it must be for her to sing about a good Heavenly Father when her only experience with an earthly father was so difficult. For Angie, this piece of her identity must've felt complicated at best.

My friend, if this is hard, I wish I could wrap my arms around you now in the way I did with Angie that day. As you explore all the pieces of who you are, I wish I could whisper in your ear that God loves you. I believe He is rejoicing that you are taking time to explore your relationship with Him. He cares for you deeply. He is calling out for you to open your heart to His love. He is your good, good Father. It's who He is and knowing that will shape who you are.

But I know that looking back at that piece of your life—that relationship with your father—can be tricky. I hope you know that, though it's an integral part of understanding who you are and Whose you

41

are, it isn't easy. So, be gentle with yourself as you consider what this might mean for you.

What was your relationship like with your dad?
How has this relationship impacted who you are today?
How has it shaped your view of God?

There was a lot of reflection around these questions in our group of Kaleidoscopes. In that group of thirty women, all of whom lived in the same community and had a broad range of jobs, we had some big differences regarding this piece of our lives. I would imagine this is true for your group of friends, too. I think that's because we're human, and a huge part of being human is recognizing the differences and complexities of our pieces.

We'll never get this relationship thing right. And you know what? Even if they're giving it their best efforts, your earthly fathers won't either. As human beings, this father/daughter relationship will always be a distorted reflection of our Heavenly Father/daughter relationship. Whether you're coming from complicated, painful, and wounded places with your father or operating out of the best possible relationship with your dad you could have, you're still going to end up with some distorted puzzle pieces.

So, what do you do? How do you reconcile this piece of who you are and Whose you are?

I find hope in an old story I once heard.

A seminary professor was vacationing with his wife in Gatlinburg, Tennessee. One morning, they ate breakfast at a little restaurant, hoping to enjoy a quiet meal. While waiting for their food, they noticed an older gentleman moving from table to table to visit with the guests.

The professor leaned over and whispered to his wife, "I hope he doesn't come over here."

Sure enough, the man did come over to their table.

"Where are you folks from?" he asked in a friendly voice.

"Oklahoma," they answered.

"Great to have you here in Tennessee," the stranger said. "What do you do for a living?"

"I teach at a seminary school," the professor replied.

"Oh, so you teach preachers how to preach, do you? Well, I've got a really great story for you."

With that, the gentleman pulled up a chair and sat down at the table with the couple. The professor groaned, thinking to himself, *Great … Just what I need—another preacher story!*

The man pointed out the restaurant window and said, "See that mountain over there? Not far from the base of that mountain, there was a boy born to an unwed mother. He had a hard time growing up because every place he went, he was always asked the same question: 'Who's your daddy?' Eventually, the boy avoided going into stores because the question hurt him badly."

Here, the man paused before continuing quietly. "When he was about twelve years old, a new preacher came to the boy's church. Of course, the boy would always go in late and slip out early to avoid hearing the question, 'Who's your daddy?' But one day, the new preacher said the benediction so fast that the boy got caught and had to walk out with the crowd. Just about the time he got to the back door, the new preacher, not knowing anything about him, put his hand on his shoulder and asked him, 'Son, who's your daddy?' The whole church got quiet. The boy could feel every eye in the church looking at him. Now everyone would finally know the answer to that question."

The professor and his wife leaned in, now eager to hear the end of the story.

"This new preacher, though, sensed the situation around him, and using discernment that only the Holy Spirit could give, he said to that scared little boy, 'Wait a minute! I know who you are. I see the family resemblance now. You are a child of God.' He patted the boy on his shoulder and said, 'Boy, you've got a great inheritance. Go and claim it.' With that, the boy smiled for the first time in a long time and walked out the door a changed person. He was never the same again. Whenever anybody asked him, 'Who's your Daddy?' he'd just tell them, 'I'm a child of God.'"

The professor responded, "That really was a great story!"

As the older man turned to leave, he said, "You know, if that new preacher hadn't told me that I was one of God's children, I probably never would have amounted to much at all."

Then, he walked away.

The seminary professor and his wife were stunned. He called the waitress over and asked, "Do you know who that man was? The one who just left that was sitting at our table?"

The waitress grinned and said, "Of course. Everybody here knows him. That's Ben Hooper. He's the former governor of Tennessee!" [1]

You don't have to look to famous people or hear stories from far away to know the impact of this truth. No matter who you are, no matter what kind of father you have on earth, no matter how distorted that piece of the puzzle of your life is, you are a reflection of a bigger Father—your Heavenly Father. When you anchor yourself in this truth of Whose you are, you can find yourself more at ease with who you are, regardless of your relationship with your earthly father.

Here are a few things you can try to help you hold fast to this truth in your life.

1. Look to God for validation.

This goes against every notion you find in culture today. Love songs, social media, the words of others—it's all telling us where to find validation. But the reality is that you will always be disappointed when it comes to other humans.

One of my Kaleidoscopes talked about the validation she craved from her father. Both her parents seemed to only appreciate sports, but she was always more interested in academics. She tried out for the soccer team, but now, she knows it was only motivated by the belief that her parents would approve of her only if she were athletic.

---

1   https://www.mountainwings.com/past/2361.htm

Another friend shared that her parents seemed most pleased when she achieved something. As a result, she's spent her adult life trying to achieve to meet their expectations, a truth she only discovered by taking a step back to examine her behaviors.

You will always be disappointed when it comes to your relationships with others. You'll never measure up, and neither will they.

If you expect to be validated by anyone else, your earthly father included, you will end up disappointed. But if you let God meet those expectations, you will be satisfied. The only person who should speak worth into who you are? The God who made you, loves you, and wants what's best for you. When you ground who you are in His words, there's a shift in not just who you are but how you experience the relationships around you, fathers included!

2. Forgive.

Let's be very clear here: Forgiveness can be hard. Like really, really hard. It asks a lot to forgive those who have wronged you, and sometimes, it can feel like you've been hurt or betrayed so badly you don't have the ability to forgive, or the other person doesn't deserve your forgiveness.

Remember that forgiving someone doesn't mean what they did is okay. It doesn't mean you have to trust that person again. It doesn't mean you have to be close in relationship with them. All it means is that you choose to heal. You decide to release the wrong done in favor of what's best for your heart.

One Kaleidoscope, who was named after her dad, recalled her parents getting a divorce when she was six years old. The visits with her dad were infrequent for the next two years until he moved out of town and completely lost contact with her. She heard nothing from him till seventeen years later when her brother found a distant relative through an online DNA database and was given a phone number for their father.

With one text, they were back in touch with their dad. At first, their conversations were surface-level as they got to know one another again. Her dad didn't even know she was married or that he was now a grandparent. But they kept talking daily in an attempt to reintroduce themselves to each other. After nearly six months, her father came for a visit. Together in person, they started having harder conversations about why he left. Emotions ran high, but thanks to his willingness to show up, my friend was able to forgive.

Fast forward another six months, and her dad abruptly stopped answering the phone again. All the work they'd done to repair the relationship was gone like that. Her emotions of abandonment came flooding back. My friend had to make the tough decision to forgive again, this time without the promise of a relationship. Through counseling, she learned she didn't have to keep reaching out only to be let down. She learned to set boundaries and to let forgiveness heal her hurts, all without inviting the relationship with her father back to the place that it was.

Recalling this experience, she talked about how hard it was to learn to love her father for where he was instead of hoping he'd get somewhere else. She simply had to accept it, forgive it, and release it.

Anger is a one-way street. But when you forgive, you get to pick your path. You get to choose healing. You get to hold on to the truth of who you are. And when the emotional burden is too heavy, remember there is a Heavenly Father who can handle all your emotions. He is there to help you forgive.

3. Be willing to get help when you need it.

Let's be honest, this is hard work. Dealing with the pieces of disappointment and pain, whether intentional or not, is hard. Of course, you need help to get through it! Help does not mean you are weak or incapable. It means you are strong enough to address a point of pain.

Kip and I committed to attend marriage counseling for the first two years of our marriage, and I am so thankful that we did. This time helped us unpack some of the baggage we both brought into the marriage and navigate being a blended family. Once, we ran into another couple we knew in the waiting room. I could see the embarrassment on my friend's face when she realized we now knew they were in therapy, too. As we talked, I said, "Don't you think the healthiest people are the ones who are here addressing their needs?" She looked shocked at the statement, but I meant it. I still mean it today!

The healthiest people I know are the ones who are strong enough to get help. The wounds you may be experiencing from the distorted pieces of your relationships with your fathers are deep. And if you want to heal them, you must be willing to get the help you need.

Think of it like cleaning out your messiest closet. It requires you to make a huge mess before you can put it all back together in a way that works better for you. Is it fun? Not really. Is it daunting? For sure. But in the end, cleaning up that mess is worth it. The same is true for your own hurts and messes in life. When willing to share what is hard, you can look beneath the surface of pain, anger, or uncertainty to sort and sift through it. Most importantly, you can put the pieces back together in a healthier way.

4. Look forward.

As my girls have grown up, we have discussed some things they feel are "unfair." Because we are a blended family, our relationship with each of our daughters has looked a little different. Our time with them seemed different because they were different people, and their needs were individual. As a blended family, we had more time with our youngest girls, Lydia and Anne Marie, than with Lauren when she was their age. Our bonus daughter Maria joined our family when she was twenty, so her relationship with us is also different. It is easy for them to compare the things they get and even how we show them love individually. As parents, we always think about what each girl needs, but what they need can differ depending on which child and the season we're in. It's different because of their unique pieces!

On the surface, this can feel unfair. So, we've had to encourage the girls to shift their focus. Instead of looking back, look forward. Instead of focusing on what they didn't get, focus on the potential of what's to come.

It is possible that you feel the relationship you had with your earthly father was a bit unfair. Though my dad was amazing, I still struggle with feelings of unfairness because I lost him so suddenly. So, if you want to throw out a "no fair," let me meet you there and encourage you to look forward, too. You have a good, good Father in God who may have something to add to your story—blessings you can't imagine just ahead.

My mother struggled with this concept for many years herself. One year, she attended a women's event where the discussion centered around the father/daughter relationship. Some of the women could not relate to God as a Father to them, so the speaker flipped the script. She suggested that if it's too hard to understand how God can be a good father because of their experiences with their earthly fathers, they could instead consider how they feel about their own children. The women with children could understand God's sacrificial parental love for us because they have felt the same way for their children, even if it was just a brief, distorted piece of the way God loves us as His children. She encouraged them to consider that God loves their children even more than they do! And with that, many of the women who, like my mother, struggled to look forward with an understanding of God as their Father began to see God as their loving parent.

My prayer for you, friend, is that this would be one of the most meaningful and beneficial exercises you engage in for yourself. That in understanding more about who you are and Whose you are, you can look forward with healing, hope, and confidence.

Who You Are

- What did you learn about yourself from your dad? How has that shaped who you are today?
- What aspects of your relationship with your dad do you want to carry with you into your other relationships? What aspects do you want to forgive and leave behind?
- Are there aspects of the relationship with your dad that need healing?

Whose You Are

- What description comes to mind as you think about God as a Father?
- God loves you unconditionally. You cannot further earn nor lose His love. How is this different or similar to your relationship with your earthly father?
- Is there something different about how you handle relationships because you believe in God? If God is not a part of your daily decisions, what would change if you believed He is with you and loves you?

A Prayer

Dear God,

Thank You that you are a good, good Father. Sometimes, my perspective of you is distorted because of my dad. Even the best fathers out there are human still, and that means there are some gaps in my heart that an earthly father can't fill. I choose to forgive my father for any missteps or hurts and to accept that, even when he failed me, You never did. Help me not view You through the distorted lens of broken humans.

Help me look through the lens of Your love and trust that You worked out all the details in my life to point me to You. I pray You are shaping who I am. Mold me into who You want me to be and help me reflect Your love to the world.

Take all my pieces and use them to point others to You.

Amen.

A Truth to Remember

*See what great love the Father has lavished on us, that we should be
called children of God! And that is what we are! The reason the world
does not know us is that it did not know him (1 John 3:1 NIV).*

CHAPTER THREE
The Piece That Is Shattered

Over the years, one of the most insightful exercises I have done with my students focuses on worry and stress. First, I have students write down their most arduous experience or most stressful event on an index card. Then, they place their card in a bowl. There are no names attached, so the stories and experiences written on each card remain anonymous. I then pass the bowl around, asking each person to randomly select a card and read aloud what was written on the one they chose.

Of course, some people blow off the exercise and write something silly, like having to mow the grass on a Saturday. But for the most part, people are surprisingly honest. I have been amazed at some of the unthinkable things I have heard in these groups.

I walked through years of infertility, including multiple surgeries, thousands of dollars, and all the emotions, only to discover that my husband had secretly had a vasectomy to prevent us from having children.

My brother suffered a seizure as a child and passed away. I was there and could not help him. I went on to a career in medicine because of it.

I was in the second tower on 9/11. I made it outside to see the building crumble with so many friends and coworkers still inside. I left New York and haven't been back since.

I had to ignite a bomb in a small town during a war. I have never told anyone about it to this day.

Remembering the power of this exercise, I asked my Kaleidoscopes to participate in it with me in preparation for this book. Though I know them well, their responses to the cards they had been dealt amazed me.

I was at the playground with my four-year-old daughter when she was hit by a falling tree. She passed away in my arms.

My husband had a yearlong affair that everyone in our community knew about the whole time.

My son was born with a rare condition that requires extensive medical treatments and a lot of hard decisions.

I was diagnosed with progressed cancer when my son was very young.

I've suffered for years from an eating disorder, and it is a daily struggle.

There is so much pain in the pieces of our stories, but you don't need me to tell you that. You know because you've lived it. You're walking with some painful pieces of your own.

However, the good news is the story doesn't have to end there. Every time I do this exercise, I close with one final question: If given the chance, would you trade what you wrote on your card for the one you hold in your hand?

More often than not, the participants decide to keep the hardship they lived through rather than trade for the card of someone else, even if it's seemingly harder than the one they selected from the bowl. I don't know anyone who would trade for the stories mentioned above. Yet I have been surprised time and time again when I hear someone say they would choose to keep the pain they've experienced, even if it is seemingly much harder than what they selected from the bowl. Why? Well, I think it's because of the lesson they learned through their hardship. Their pain became a piece of who they are, for better or worse. And for many, if that pain was dealt with and acknowledged in a real, healthy way, it made them stronger. It became a piece of who they are and impacted how they understand Whose they are.

I know this from the classes I've taught, but I have also witnessed it in the lives of my Kaleidoscopes. From the friends whose hardships were so painful, I wouldn't dare trade my card for their own. I wouldn't switch places. I don't even have a measuring stick for what they've walked through, and yet, I have watched them push forward with a grace and strength that has changed them.

If I'm being honest, bearing witness to it has changed me, too.

One of those friends is Erin. As she approached her fortieth birthday, the desire to become a mother was unshakable. She wasn't married or in a relationship, so she knew she'd have to do it on her own if she wanted to pursue parenthood in this phase of her life. So, Erin decided to adopt a child.

She worked extra shifts as a nurse practitioner, met with a coun-selor to make sure her heart was ready to parent a child on her own, and prayed a lot. She felt completely at peace about the adoption agency she went with and the country she selected. Eventually, she was matched with a beautiful two-year-old girl from China. We cele-brated big after that. I'm talking baby showers, nursery set ups, day-care searches, shopping, and more. It was a huge moment for Erin, and friends came to support her in every way we could.

Until everything changed.

Erin was scheduled to pick up her daughter just weeks after COVID-19 shut down the world. What was supposed to be a short wait turned into a year. Eventually, two years went by without Erin bring-ing home her daughter. She prayed, she waited, but the day did not come. She was arguably in the hardest season she had ever faced pro-fessionally, working in the medical field during the pandemic. With that, she was also waiting for a child who became a more distant hope with each passing day.

During the wait, Erin tried to stay distracted. To help put her mind elsewhere, I begged her to try online dating. She declined but, unbe-knownst to me, quietly completed a profile. There, she chose to iden-tify herself as a mother because, in her heart, she was. As luck would have it, she matched with a wonderful man. A man who was a father himself. A man who reached out to her because he was open to some-one who had children. A man who loved that she was a mother.

Erin and Dave were married in one of the sweetest ceremonies of love I have ever witnessed. Dave's daughter stood next to them as they said their vows, making Erin a mother through their marriage. It wasn't her perfect ending. In fact, finally finding the man to be a father to the child she was waiting on made the wait harder in some ways. But still, there was beauty, even in the pain.

I have walked with Erin through the excitement, the waiting, the questions, the anger, and the pain. Ultimately, the changed adoption restrictions during the wait meant that Erin would not get to bring her daughter home. When we discovered that, I asked her, "What do you need to do?"

Her response was simple and profound.

"I just have to accept it."

To accept the pain of our unmet expectations is something no one would willingly choose, but it's something you have to do, nonetheless. This just isn't how it was *supposed* to be, is it?

He wasn't *supposed* to die.
I was *supposed* to have kids.
We were *supposed* to grow old together.
She wasn't *supposed* to quit.

Yes, accepting unmet expectations is hard. And pain, while inevitable, is also hard. I heard it said differently at the funeral of my uncle, who passed away too soon. A wise friend of our family hugged my cousin as she wept and said, "It has to be."

So, I meet you here, in the moment of "it has to be." It hurts. Pain is real, and some pain will not change. It becomes a piece of who you are. And perhaps, even harder, it becomes a piece of the way you see Whose you are. Because in the pain, as you long to hear from God, sometimes it feels like the silence is deafening.

In the pain, the wait can be agonizing.

When I was in labor with Anne Marie, the wait for her felt excruciating at times. Once my parents arrived at the hospital, I invited them to come into the room to see that I was okay. As luck would have it, that's when things really took off. My dad was standing next to me as things began to progress quickly, and I started shaking uncontrollably. Dad left the room, struggling to see me like that. I later learned that he went to the waiting room and wept at the sight of me in so much pain.

My friend, I need to tell you that I believe God responds much the same when He sees us suffering. God weeps with us in our pain, too. Scripture tells us Jesus was a "man of sorrows and acquainted with grief."[2] When Mary and Martha met Jesus following the death of their brother Lazarus, Jesus wept.[3] Not because He couldn't fix it (He did!), but because He saw their pain. He was empathetic. He cared. And I think you have to remember that the same is true for you in your pain today. Jesus is still here, always loving you and likely weeping alongside you as you carry your shattered pieces.

Yet again, there is good news here. Yes, you must pause in your pain. You must feel it, grieve it, live it. But, with God, you can look forward with hope. With God, your pain isn't the end of the story. In fact, it's only the beginning.

When handed over to God, there can be purpose in the shattered pieces of your pain.

---

2   Isaiah 53:3
3   John 11:35

One of my dear friends, Lisa, leads our church group. Together, we walked through the passing of her father from lung cancer. What I didn't know was that my own dad would unexpectedly pass away just one month later. The grief process has so many ups and downs, but Lisa has been one month ahead of me every step of the way. She gave purpose to the pain of losing her father by walking with me through the loss of mine. Together, we navigated the shattered pieces of grief.

Perhaps this is part of God's plan for your pain. Maybe part of your healing is finding the ability to reach back and carry someone else toward their own. It can make pain feel purposeful when you share it with someone who needs to learn from your experience. When you turn your shattered pieces over to Whose you are, you find a new sense of who you are, pain and all.

People tend to think that our shattered pieces are unique. That our pain is specific to us. But remember my friend, all tears taste of salt. Deep pain is a shared part of the human experience, but it is in this shared experience that God meets us. It is in this space that an understanding of how God can use our pain for a purpose takes roots. When you share your pain with Him, you will find the strength to share it with others who need to know they aren't alone in picking up their shattered pieces.

So, hold tight to those pieces. Trust them to Whose you are. God may be using what feels like a breakdown for a breakthrough; you just can't see it yet. He may have your past in mind for a purpose you can't picture. The pain you are experiencing today is real, but that doesn't mean God isn't working and weeping in the midst of it.

Remember the promise in Romans 8:28 (NIV):

And we know that in all things, God works for the good of those who love him, who have been called according to his purpose.

The One intimately aware of our unique challenges can use them for good. This pain is not the end because God is still working all things for His good.

So, what can you do as you hold these shattered pieces and wait for God to make them good? How can you walk through your pain in a way that changes who you are for the better and helps you find purpose in trusting Whose you are with the rest?

Here's where I think you can start!

1. Acknowledge that your pain is real.

Whether you are dealing with pain from long ago or currently walking through it, the first step is to get real about what you feel. Be honest with yourself. Bring it out into the open. You can't begin to put our pieces back together if you aren't willing to acknowledge them in the first place. So, you've got to recognize the very real weight of your pain to start.

One of my Kaleidoscopes went through years of fertility treatments. Day after day, I saw her try to smile through her pain. One day, I asked her how she was doing, and with tears streaming down her face, she told me she was doing "good." Rather than let her continue without acknowledging her genuine pain, I simply replied, "You know, it's okay to say today sucks."

I'd give the same advice to you! It's okay to name what hurts you. It's okay to say it out loud. It's okay to stop hiding the fact that you are hurting. Sometimes, the only way to mend a broken heart is to let it fall apart. It's okay to say your pain is real. In fact, you must be willing to name it so that you can move forward in it.

2. The toughies are your teachers.

This is another of my dad's many mantras in life. In any hardship, he would remind me, "April, the toughies are our teachers." Man, it hurts to hear, but it sure is true.

Learn from the hard knocks.
Learn from the pain.
Learn you can handle much more than you thought.
Learn you're stronger when you endure.

You have to ask yourself: What can I do with the cards I have been dealt? What am I willing to learn from this tough circumstance? What can I discover about who I am and Whose I am from the pain I'm walking through?

I've been friends with Rachel for thirty years. In that time, I came to know and love her family as well. So, it was a shock to us all when her mother was diagnosed with terminal lung cancer. Her mother, Sandra, was a shining example of looking at a challenging circumstance as an opportunity to teach others how to grow in their faith. Her pain reminded her how fleeting life is and how imperative it is for us to use our time for good.

Rather than wallow, Sandra made it her mission to share the love of Christ up until her final day. For weeks, she even planned with the pastor who would share the message at her service, not about her own life, but rather about the love of Jesus. There was pain, yes, but there was also beauty in her resolve to lean into Christ through it. Rachel was changed by witnessing her mom face death with grace and strength.

We all were.

Really, that is often where change begins to happen—through the 'toughies' that can be your teachers if you allow them to make you better rather than bitter.

3. Embrace the AND.

It makes me feel sad when I hear people feel guilty about the pain they're carrying. Hear me say, my friend, that God can handle our AND. It's okay for us to feel two things at one time. It's okay for us to carry the weight of our pain *and* still go forward in our lives.

One of my favorite gifts to share with someone in pain is the "&" symbol. It's a way to help them remember that it's okay to experience several emotions simultaneously. It's a reminder of the importance of AND.

In our pain, you can be ...

Scared AND strong.
Sad AND thankful.
Angry AND hopeful.
Afraid AND still trust God.
Have questions about the future AND find peace in moments.
Pray for more time AND treasure the day.
Weary AND hopeful.

Let me add here that the AND is valid in all seasons. It is possible to cherish your children AND be exhausted by them. You may be grateful for another work opportunity AND be overwhelmed by starting a new job. You can be excited to try something new AND scared of the new things ahead. You can be in pain AND still believe there is purpose in what you're walking through.

You learn that you can handle a lot more than you thought you could.

4. Remember God is with you.

When things are going well, it is easy to forget God is with you. And when things are hard, it is easy to doubt God is with you. In short, it's easy in any season to forget God's presence is *always* available, especially in your pain.

Once, I was teaching a class on worry and stress when a man walked up to me at the end. He was so calm and resolved as he waited for everyone else to finish talking with me before he asked his question.

In a whisper, he asked, "What if you already know the outcome, and it is bad?"

I knew what he was talking about because some of his co-workers had given me a heads up; His wife had recently received a diagnosis of terminal cancer. Now, he was in the waiting room of his life. This is where my job in corporate training can get tricky because I am not supposed to speak about faith. I broke the rules that day because I didn't know how to approach this level of pain without the One who already knows the outcome. I can't navigate hardship without leaning on God's presence.

The outcome may not change depending on your reaction, but you have two choices: Experience pain with God or experience it without Him.

My friend, I pray you choose the first option.

5. Treat everyone you meet as though their heart is breaking.

It is essential to acknowledge that, just as real as your pain is, there are hurting people all around you, too. Every interaction is an opportunity for you to encourage others. Every encounter is a chance for you to point a hurting soul back to the God who loves them. Every moment is a chance to find purpose in your own pain.

One day, when I was a teenager, my mom drove us to a Christmas tree farm. Our house was already decorated, so I didn't understand why we were shopping for a Christmas tree. To my surprise, my mom picked out a tree, just not for our home. I remember my mom digging through the car looking for a scrap piece of paper to attach to the tree just before she dropped it on our neighbor's doorstep. On that scrap paper, she simply wrote, "Love, Santa."

Several years passed before the neighbor acknowledged the importance of that gift. She eventually told my mom, "I know that was you, but what you don't know is that I was thinking of ending my life that night. You gave me a reason to make it through just one more holiday."

The person in the drive-thru line,
the one in front of you at carpool,
your waiter or waitress,
the friend who texts you late at night ...

Remember, these are people carrying their shattered pieces. You are uniquely positioned to breathe fresh hope and life into their circumstances.

I hope you know that despite the shattered pieces, your story isn't finished. You may feel broken, but that doesn't mean healing isn't happening. God knows your deepest wounds. God understands your trauma. God knows how unfair life feels right now. God is weeping, working, and with you every step of the way.

Your pain may be the beginning of discovering more about who you are and Whose you are. My prayer for you, friend, is that today will be the day you see your shattered pieces as the beginning of a bigger story.

A story only God can write.

Who You Are

- How do you typically deal with pain?
- What pain can you look back on and see that it helped shape who you are today?
- What pain are you currently facing?
- How is that pain impacting your life daily?

Whose You Are

- Have you ever experienced God, even in the middle of hard circumstances? How so?
- How does knowing that God feels your pain and weeps with you in it make you feel?

- Can you even imagine how God might use the pain you have experienced or are currently experiencing to fulfill His purpose?

A Prayer

Dear God,

Thank You that You don't shy away from my pain. Instead, You invite me to bring it to You. Thank You for making everything beautiful in its time. Please forgive my doubt and impatience. I know You are at work, even when I can't see it. I know You are present, and I know that You care. Help me to trust that You are never late and always working all things for my good. I believe Your plan is still good. I know You can be trusted. Remind me of Your goodness, even now.

Help me look through the lens of Your love and trust that You will use the pain and the joy in life to point me to You. I pray You are shaping who I am. Mold me into who You want me to be and help me reflect Your love to the world.

Take all my pieces and use them to point others to You.

Amen.

A Truth to Remember

He has made everything beautiful in its time. He has also set eternity in the human heart; yet no one can fathom what God has done from beginning to end (Ecclesiastes 3:11 NIV).

CHAPTER FOUR
The Connected Piece

By my twenty-sixth birthday, most of my friends were getting married, and I was already going through the big D: divorce.

The whole experience made me question so much about myself.

Was I someone who could be loved?
How could I not doubt every single part of who I thought I was?
Had I already ruined my chance of having a family of my own before I hit thirty?

The whole thing wrecked a core belief I had about marriage: That only people who didn't try hard enough got a divorce. Suddenly, I realized that wasn't true. Now, I checked a box I always wanted to avoid. Now, I was part of a statistic I never thought possible for me. I didn't know how I got so lost, so off track. Maybe I should have taken that left turn in Albuquerque because here, in this reality, something was horribly amiss.

To say I felt alone would be an understatement. I moved back into the safety net of my parents' home and spent Saturdays with my two dogs, Cody and Calvin. Friends were calling to check on me, but the rhythm of my phone buzzing seemed to dwindle as the days went by. Eventually, I signed up for email newsletters and shopping text threads just so I could hear the ding.

And let me tell you, when your job is to help other people navigate their relationships, and your personal life is falling apart, it's more than a little awkward. There was one night I specifically remember during this season. I arrived at a community center to teach a Dale Carnegie Course, and the room was decorated for a wedding that was to occur that weekend. Talk about a blow to my wounded and tender heart! To make matters worse, the session topic that night was relationships. There I was, newly divorced and standing under the bridal arch set up for the weekend's ceremony, teaching other people how to have successful relationships.

Yes, it was as bad as it sounds.

I felt like a complete counterfeit. I was in front of businesspeople teaching how to get along well with others, and I couldn't even make it work at home. The whole thing felt like an exclamation point on my failure.

I've heard it said that the teacher will appear when the student is ready. Well, somewhere in my turmoil, I decided to become a student of the material all over again. I recommitted to learning what I was teaching in my classes, and this time, I saw the content entirely differently. Now, I was viewing it all not through a lens of success or failure but through a lens of compassion and understanding for my students, their stories, and all our complex and complicated relationships.

As it turns out, relationships are complex, wonderful, and constantly changing. Whether it's a relationship with a spouse or significant other, a family member, a coworker, a friend, or just a neighbor we cross paths with occasionally, we don't always appreciate the complexity or influence these relationships have on the pieces of who we are. We don't always see how they shape not just how we see who we are but how we see who others are, too.

Relationships are complex. They're made up of people who are flawed and imperfect, and we will inevitably get it wrong a time or two. And that means they likely deserve way more work and attention than we give them. After all, relationships can influence who we become. They leave a permanent tattoo on our skin, our personality, and our ability to have other relationships. They're strong enough to give us a common bond yet powerful enough to tear us apart.

But you don't need me to tell you this, do you? You experience the complexity of relationships in your life regularly.

I mean, even science is backing us up here. Social psychologists have claimed that our identity is often shaped by what we think other people think of us. If the people we're in relationship with label us as beautiful, we believe it. We hold on to that if they say we're smart, personable, or athletic. We think it about ourselves. We let it become a piece of who we are.

When Kip and I started dating, he repeatedly said, "You are beautiful." It made me so uncomfortable because I didn't feel beautiful on the inside or the outside. I was broken in so many ways that it was hard to believe I could be seen as anything other than that: broken. Still, he persisted with praise. He came to my office and learned about my work, got to know my friends, spent time with my family, and discovered what I enjoyed. He saw who I was, even though I had forgotten. And eventually, I began to believe him. I started to see myself as he saw me: whole and worthy of love.

Of course, the bad news is that the same is true for the negative labels. If someone tells us we're wrong, unkind, unworthy, or not good enough, we start to believe it. We often hold on to the bad despite our best efforts, so much so that those labels become pieces of who we think we are, too.

I believe relationships shape who we are because our experiences with people form our perspectives. It is often said, "We are a product of our circumstances." It could also be said, "We are a product of our relationships." And that's why, in a conversation about identity, I think it's essential to look at the relationships in our lives. Because, for better or worse, our relationships can impact our understanding of identity—who we are and Whose we are.

So, what do you do? If relationships are part of life (and they are), how do you approach them in a way that helps you and the other person? If they can impact your life, how do you ensure you're handling them in a healthy way?

While I don't have all the correct answers, I can tell you where I think you need to begin: With yourself. I heard pastor and speaker Andy Stanley put it this way: "What is it like on the other side of me?" In other words, what are you contributing to your relationships—the good, the bad, and everything in between? Before you can focus on how the relationships in your life impact you, I think you have to consider how you're impacting them.

So, take a real, honest look at your different relationships. What patterns do you see yourself contributing to over and over again?

Do you have long-lasting friendships with very little drama?
Or are most of your friendships up and down with fights and volatility?

Do you tend to give more than you take?
Or do you tend to get more than you give?

Do you have a lot of friends?
Or do you like to keep your circle tight?

Do you tend to let people go too quickly?
Or do you want to hang on too long?

Do you become angry and react quickly?
Or do you find yourself letting go and moving on easily?

Do you make time to pour into the people in your life?
Or do you expect to be on the receiving end of their energy more often than not?

I know this isn't easy. When I consider how I show up to the relationships in my life, some of my answers to these questions hit hard. You have to remember that the common denominator in your relationships is … well, you. If you're not putting the best pieces of who you are into your relationships, how can you expect the same from someone else? While you can't change others, you can change yourself. So maybe, today, that's where you start. If we're all connected pieces in life's bigger puzzle, I think you must first focus on handling your own pieces. You must think about who *you* are in relationship first.

I then think it's key to remember Whose you are. As a Christian, there is no relationship more valuable than the one you have with God. It's the one that not only shapes who you are, but how you enter into relationships with others.

Think about it! If your relationship with God is in the right place, aren't you better able to handle the ups and downs of other relationships? It's easier to resolve a fight with my husband when I walk closely with God, who gives me the grace to apologize and forgive. I'm more patient with my children when spending time with God, who grants patience. I'm a better friend when I'm experiencing God as a friend to me. The list could go on and on.

The point? When you lean into your relationship with Whose you are, how you respond to and engage in the rest of your relationships shows it. You let go of expectations because you know the only one who will ultimately fulfill you is your Heavenly Father. You choose to make someone else feel welcome, seen, heard, valued, loved, and supported. You walk securely in your identity no matter what's happening around you. And that means you're stepping into every relationship—the good, the bad, the ugly, the mediocre—with an unshakeable sense of confidence in who you are and Whose you are.

The good relationships? They'll be better for it. And the tricky, complex, or just downright hard relationships? Well, they'll have less power to impact the pieces of ourselves that matter most.

So, to ensure our relationships impact us for good, let's focus on trying a few things.

1. Identify the critical relationships that have shaped who you are today.

Allow me to get you started on this journey here by prompting you to think intentionally about your relationships. Who are the key relationships in your life? Take time to list the first ten people who come to mind. Then, think about how those relationships have influenced you, for good and not-so-good.

What have you learned about yourself from this person?
How does the relationship make you feel?
What does it encourage you to believe about yourself?
Does this relationship draw you closer to God or pull you further away?

My relationship with my grandmother considerably shaped me. I respected the way she loved people so much. We were always close, but I never really realized how much I was like her until I was at her celebration of life. As each person stood to tell stories, I heard pieces of myself in each one. The way she collected people in her life. The way she valued her family. She always had a bunch of people gathered around her kitchen table, even though she didn't cook. This is me! Her influence was vital in shaping many pieces of who I am, big and small.

So, who is on your list? Who are the key people in your life? And how have they influenced you?

Now, if you're feeling brave, I'd encourage you to take this exercise a step further. Look at that list and ask yourself: *What would these people say about how I influence them?*

In other words, how are you contributing to their lives through your relationship with them? Some answers may be encouraging and helpful, but if you're honest, you'd probably have to admit that you aren't always getting it right. That's because you're a person, too! And as a person dealing with another person, there's always room to improve.

2. Invest in the people you love.

Consider where you're investing and putting your time into those key relationships in your life. Of course, as I said, the primary relationship you need to invest in is your relationship with God. But beyond that, which relationships are you investing the most time and effort in now?

Your relationship with your spouse?
Your kids?
Your coworkers?
Your small group?
Your friends?
Your family members?

Where is the majority of your effort going? It's an important question to consider because it shows you which relationships matter to you right now. Look at your calendar for the next month and ask yourself some questions:

Who do I make time for in my schedule?
Is my time spent focusing on the people and relationships that matter most?

I decided to start a Bible study for Lydia's friends on Friday afternoons. This means coordinating schedules and snacks with other moms and planning our time together. I wanted to get to know my daughters' friends, and I believed that investing in them was an investment in the person Lydia would one day become. I believed scheduling time to focus on the right things with these girls was a worthy investment of my time. Is it always convenient? No. Can I see the fruits now? Hardly. But was it worth it? Absolutely!

3. Remember the give and take.

This one may be difficult, but it's essential. When it comes to your relationships, you must consider that there is a time to give and a time to receive. There are seasons to relationships, and you have to be open-handed and open-hearted as they ebb and flow.

When I began my research for writing this book, my Kaleidoscopes showed up to help me gather ideas. They had nothing to gain from this gathering, yet they were still willing to support me. During this season, I received, and I pray for the day I can give back to them in a way they need.

When I work with students at Lydia's Place, they're often in survival mode. They can do nothing but receive from us, and that's okay! In the season of relationships there, I show up to pour out without expecting the students to give anything to me in return.

Maybe you're in a season that requires you to receive a lot from other people right now. Or maybe you're in a place where you have more to give. This is all part of the cycle of relationships, and if you pay attention to it, you'll notice how the seasons change. There are times you join a church group because you need to learn, and there are times when you're called to help others grow in their faith. There are times you are the support system for your friends, and there are times when you're the friend being supported. There are times when you're the spouse keeping things going at home, and there are times when you need your spouse to run the show.

In relationships—familial, platonic, and romantic—there will always be a give and take. For a relationship to work, you must approach it with the attitude of what you can offer them, not how you can gain from it. In God's family, you don't always give and take the same amount in each relationship simultaneously. Giving to someone who can't give back to me in the same capacity keeps my motives in check. And when I am the beneficiary of a blessing from someone who doesn't owe me, it is humbling and keeps me grateful.

4. Vote with your feet.

My dad always told me you "vote with your feet." In other words, you show up. That's a huge part of operating as a connected piece of a larger relationship puzzle.

After my dad passed, my uncle James shared a fond memory he had of my dad with me. My dad was on a work trip in Massachusetts when my aunt, James' wife, had a heart attack. My dad left his work trip and flew all the way to Texas to visit my uncle in the hospital, even though we lived in Georgia at the time. James recalled looking up in the hospital to see my dad walking down the hall. He was shocked that my dad had dropped everything to show up, but that's what my dad did; he voted with his feet. He showed up.

People remember when you do the same.

When I felt the nudge to start a prayer group to talk about foster care and help kids who were aging out, I called random women in my community who were also involved in foster care work. These women were not my closest friends; I barely even knew many of them, but I got connected to them through a fellow friend who was in the middle of an adoption journey. My friend, Heather, graciously agreed to open her home to host a prayer night for myself and the women I'd invited. She cleaned her home, ordered the food, and even arranged a babysitter for the night. She put a lot of effort into the preparations, and when I arrived, we each took a deep breath of excitement about the night ahead.

We waited for the doorbell to ring.

And it never did.

Not one single person showed up, and I was devastated. Of course, Heather could see my embarrassment. I was even more bothered that I'd put her through so much trouble for nothing. When I told her as much, her response floored me.

"Well, we said this was a prayer night, and here we are. So, let's pray."

There, in the quiet of her home, Heather prayed with me. It wasn't the big gathering I'd hoped it would be, but in many ways, it was better. As we closed our time in prayer together, she looked at me intently and said, "I don't know where this is all going, but I want you to know that I am committed to praying you through it."

That simple act of faith and friendship changed me. Heather showed up for me, and I've never forgotten how it made me feel.

Years later, when my dad passed away suddenly, another Heather in my life did the same. She didn't send the obligatory "Let me know how I can help" message. She did me one better.

"I'm here to serve," she said in a text. "Put me to work!"

So, I did. I put her in charge of decorating an entire fellowship hall for my dad's celebration of life. In a matter of about three texts, she took my ideas and made them all happen. I walked into the service that day and saw every detail done just how I'd hoped.

This simple act of service allowed me to focus on grief and be present for my family. It changed how I reach out to friends when I hear of their hardships. It showed me the value of showing up.

5. Open your circle.

One of the beautiful things about the way God created His people for relationship is the opportunity it gives us to meet, invest in, and grow with new people all the time. You may cross paths with people who benefit from a relationship with you or vice versa! But in order to get to know them, you have to open your circles. You have to expand your horizons to make room for new people and new relationships.

In my mom's collection of kaleidoscopes, each one looks different. On the outside, one is made from a Coke bottle, another looks like a child's plastic toy, while others are more formal, decorative pieces. Of course, they don't just look different on the exterior. On the inside, they are made of so many different random elements: Seashells, broken glass, beads, and even marbles. It is the variety that makes the patterns interesting.

In the same way, it is the different people in our lives who make life rich. Try to include people with different backgrounds and beliefs in your circle. Look for the people who look different than you, who make you think, who share new ideas. Share life with people who are not your same age or stage because you can learn from them or pull them along. You will find it richer when there is a blend of ideas.

Every year at the start of the school year, my girls' big concern is always if they'll have a friend in their class. As an adult, I do the same thing. I want to try a new gym but question whether I should go alone. I want to join a small group but won't know anyone else in the room. I want to go to that party but don't want to go alone. When this comes up, my girls and I always have the same conversation—one that helps me just as much as it helps them! Instead of just thinking about the friends you already have, look for the people who need a friend. Choose to be a friend to make a friend.

Kip teaches me this all the time. Once, I asked him how he finds a way to connect with everyone he meets. He replied, "I just make up my mind before I meet someone new that I am going to like them." Then, he stays in the conversation until he finds something that connects the two of them together. In other words, Kip goes into every encounter with eyes to open his circle to others.

I recognize that this is easier said than done for many of us. Sometimes, even with our best efforts, the circle of people in our lives just can't seem to expand. If that's the place you're in, let me just encourage you with this truth: God is already in your circle. If you're walking with Him, you're already in the most impactful relationship possible. So, as you seek to open your circle to others, ask God for help, provision, and courage. I promise you He won't disappoint!

John Croyle, a mentor of mine in the world of foster care, says, "Show me your friends, and I'll show you your future." In other words, relationships matter. Each person in our life has the ability to impact who you are now and who you are becoming. They have the power to shape the way you experience the truth of Whose you are. They are important, connected pieces of the world God made.

They're essential pieces of you.

Who You Are

- What do you think the experience is like for people you are around? What is it like on the other side of you?
- When you think of your relationships, who are you most free to be yourself with?
- Is there a person you need to work on a relationship with? Is there a relationship you need to build or repair? Is there a relationship that you need to let go of?

Whose You Are

- Reflect on a time when a relationship here on earth impacted how you saw God or your relationship with Him.
- What relationships do you have that make you feel closer to Whose you are now? How do they do this?
- When the people in your life reflect on their relationship with you, what do you suspect they might say about how you pull them closer to God?
- How might you better help others understand God's love in the way you love them?

A Prayer

Dear God,

Your word says iron sharpens iron. Help me be one who not only sharpens but also one who is willing to be sharpened. Help me see others as valuable and, therefore, treat them with dignity. Help me resist the temptation to view relationships as a way to benefit myself but rather as an opportunity to serve. Please forgive me for the times I have caused pain in others, and please help me forgive. Help me spot the goodness You bring into my life through other people.

Help me look through the lens of Your love and trust that You worked out all of the relationships in my life to point me to You. I pray You are shaping who I am. Mold me into who You want me to be and help me reflect Your love to the world.

Take all of my pieces and use them to point others to You.

Amen.

A Truth to Remember

As iron sharpens iron, so one person sharpens another (Proverbs 27:17 NIV).

CHAPTER FIVE
The Piece You Believe In

As a child, I loved Santa Claus. Like most children, I got caught up in the magic of Christmas and the anticipation that Ol' Saint Nick would come down my chimney to leave presents made especially for me. What more could a kid want than the promise of presents waiting for them when they opened their eyes on Christmas morning?

I'm not ashamed to tell you that I believed in the magic well past the age I probably should have. That is until the Christmas when my brother, who is four years younger than me, decided to take matters into his own hands. That year, he encouraged me to sneak down the stairs in the middle of the night and try to catch a glimpse of the legend himself. So, I did just that! As I crept down the stairs, I was shocked to find my parents dressed in pajamas, wearily placing gifts around the tree.

I was devastated. I had believed. Oh, how I believed! I believed like a child. I believed in Santa Claus, the Tooth Fairy, and the Easter Bunny. If we'd had an Elf on the Shelf back then, I'm confident I would have also bought that hook, line, and sinker. As an adult, it's just a silly memory, but on the stairs that Christmas night, it was a shifting and shattering of my beliefs.

Perhaps you've found yourself in a similar position as an adult—a place where a long-held belief unraveled right before your eyes.

You question the faith of your childhood.
You discover your own political preferences or world views that may differ from those of your parents.
You realize bad things do happen to good people.
You see that marriage doesn't always lead to happily ever after.
You hear the terrible diagnosis and understand you are not immune.
You learn that the car of your dreams doesn't fulfill you the way you hoped.
You find out that people aren't always what they seem.
You discover the hard way that you can't change someone else.
You grasp that there is no promise your child will outlive you.
You understand that just because you expected it, it doesn't mean it will happen.
You sit helplessly as you internalize that medical technology doesn't always lead to healing.
You find that your job does not align with your passion.
You comprehend that hard work doesn't always pay off.

As you broaden your circle and world, some beliefs no longer fit. Perhaps it is an experience that shifts your perspective. Perhaps it's new information or a new person in our life. No matter how it happens, the shifting in beliefs is challenging. When you have heard something over and over again, it often feels factually incorrect when new information or a different perspective is presented. It is hard to accept it. Why? Well, because if you let go of this belief, you must wonder which others you'll be forced to let go of next.

Why am I asking you to think about every belief you've had to doubt, question, or change along the way? Well, because, whether you realize it or not, your beliefs shape your identity. They have a way of impacting your understanding of who you are and Whose you are. And that makes developing a solid set of beliefs a pretty big deal!

So, let's back it up for a second. What are beliefs? They're assumptions you make about the world. They're the tenets or convictions that people hold to be true. I have beliefs, and you have beliefs. Beliefs are tricky because they're not something we're born with. Instead, they're things you inherit, take in, or develop. Most people play around with different beliefs before adopting them as their own. They take them in, toss them around in their minds, and negotiate with them. And once a belief forms in their heart, it becomes a part of their identity.

Typically, beliefs get introduced in two ways: through relationships and experiences. Relationally, beliefs can be introduced by friends or family—the people in your circle. See why relationships are important in discovering who you are and Whose you are? Because beliefs are contagious. Most tend to adopt the beliefs of the people around them. For example, if you live in the South, you may have no concept of church not being a staple in a community. If you go to a college with strong political stances that attract other students with the same views, you may adopt them as well. If you are in a relationship and trust the other person, your viewpoints often merge and shift to include their beliefs.

Rather than tell you this is true—that our relationships and experiences shape our beliefs—I'll let my Kaleidoscopes show you how this has played out in their lives. When I asked them how their beliefs impacted their lives, for better or worse, this is what they had to say.

"As a child, my dad was in and out of jail, and it was embarrassing, so much so that I believed I had to be better than everyone else in school so no one would notice me."

"To get positive attention, I had to be perfect. Do the right activities, be friends with the right people, get the best grades, be athletic, be polite, win the awards, marry the right guy, wear the right clothes. That's how I got approval from Mom and Dad."

"My parents were divorced, and I had to constantly measure what I was saying and who I was pleasing to keep peace."

"I believed I wasn't college material, so I had to take a job I didn't like because I wasn't good enough for anything else."

"I had to be super successful because I didn't graduate high school."

"I had to stay married to keep my friends, or make my children happy, or because my family would disown me if not."

"I had to be in church every time the doors were open. I had to earn God's love."

"I had to be a stay-at-home mom because that is what my mom did for me."

See what I mean? The beliefs you hold on to are powerful pieces! They have the potential to shape not just what you believe about who you are but every step you take after that, too.

Of course, beliefs can (and often do!) change along the way. As you change and grow, your beliefs typically do the same. Some beliefs need to change with time and experience. You can look back in history to see when entire communities or nations operated from a belief they were convinced was true then, only to realize later it wasn't.

People worshipped the sun as their god, only for science to advance, and it was discovered the sun was nothing more than hydrogen and helium.

People believed communities should be segregated and separated by race and class for the good of the community, only to find their prejudices and discriminations were based on hate and lies.

People believed smoking wasn't harmful and could even be beneficial—there were even doctor-recommended brands! —only for research to discover the danger.

The list could go on and on. The point is that beliefs often motivate you to act, and if you're not carefully examining those beliefs, you may find yourself acting in a way you never thought you would. For better or worse, your beliefs motivate your behaviors, thoughts, and choices. So, when faced with a belief you're not sure is serving you anymore, you're left with a choice: You can change your beliefs, or your beliefs can change you.

During my sophomore year in college, I had it all together by all outward appearances. I was making good grades, working as a campus tour guide, a member of a sorority, and going on a summer study abroad trip to London. But while I was away on that trip, it felt like everything fell apart back home. My dad had a massive stroke, causing him to lose his short-term memory and vision; a friend passed away on a mission trip; my cousin, who grew up with me, moved to the streets, and my grandfather was placed in a memory care facility.

I was hearing all the news from across the pond, and there wasn't a single thing I could do to change any of it. I was so overwhelmed in a new place surrounded by new people that I couldn't even find words to express my feelings. So, I internalized it all. The result? I became slowly convinced something terrible would happen to me, too.

Just like that, it became a belief.

It sounds crazy now, but my mind was locked in fear at the time. Unfortunately, I brought that fear-based belief home with me. And eventually, it spiraled completely out of control, affecting every choice, thought, and behavior during that season.

I would pull up to a traffic light and sit locked in fear, unsure of which way to turn to avoid the fatal car accident my belief told me was on the way. I lay in bed at night with absolute certainty that lightning would come through the roof and strike me dead. I quit planning for anything in the future because I was convinced I wouldn't be around. If it sounds terrible, that's because it was!

Having had enough of living life like this, I found myself in the school counselor's office. She ultimately determined that I needed more help than she could provide, so she referred me to a psychiatrist. After a session, testing, and more, I was diagnosed with bipolar disorder. Mental health, in general, has a stigma, but the bipolar diagnosis felt especially shocking to me. With this newfound diagnosis, I adopted a new belief: Something is wrong with me, and I need to cover it up.

The doctor's office was on the main road in the small town where I went to school, so I always parked across the complex in front of a different building to ensure no one knew where I was going. I started taking medications and worked hard in therapy, including going to the funeral home and planning my own funeral, sitting on a grave for an entire therapy appointment, and even holding a dead frog from the science lab for an hour while talking about my fear. Of course, I did all of this without telling anyone outside my closest circle.

In privacy, I read any information I could get my hands on about coping with my condition. In my research, I read that rash decisions, unstable relationships, unemployment, as well as addiction and substance abuse are common among people who are diagnosed with bipolar disorder. Again, if it sounds like a lot, it's because it was! Based on my diagnosis and the information I found, I formed a whole new belief system about who I was going to be, but it certainly wasn't going to be someone who fell into any of the categories I'd read about in my research. Instead, I became determined to do everything in my power to do different and change my future.

Then and there, I decided ...

I would never make a major decision without someone else because I believed I couldn't be trusted on my own.
I would be a good, consistent friend to anyone who would have me because I believed this would prove I was dependable.
I would get married and stay married forever, no matter what, because I believed this would be a sign of my stability.
I would be a good student and get a good job where I would work through retirement because I believed this would show the world I could be stable and successful.

See what I mean about beliefs motivating our choices?

By the time I turned twenty-four, I'd collected a group of friends, gotten married, bought a house, and found a job at a hospital. I was doing everything that the diagnosis said I wouldn't be able to do well.

And I was absolutely miserable.

It was only after a couple of years into this outwardly shiny life I had worked so hard to create for myself that I found myself attending counseling twice a week, once for myself and once for my marriage. I knew divorce was imminent, but I wasn't going down without a fight. In an effort to save my marriage, I had lost most of my friends, and while my job was going well, I dreaded showing up each day. Still taking my medication regularly, I was struggling to understand why things weren't getting better. So, I scheduled an appointment with my doctor to address some of my concerns. After some more testing and even more talking, he sat down, looked me right in the eye, and said something that changed everything.

"April, I'm becoming concerned that we aren't dealing with bipolar disorder. You aren't cycling like I would expect, given what is going on in your life right now, so I would like to do some additional bloodwork."

Within a month, I was given a new diagnosis: a severe thyroid condition. I came off all the medications and had my thyroid removed. Physically and emotionally, I felt great. It was like I was myself again. You'd think all of this would come as a relief to me, but if I'm being honest, it didn't. I'd spent years with a belief system centered around the initial diagnosis. I let it become so much more than a diagnosis; I made it a core part of my identity. I made every decision in my life based on the beliefs that came from that diagnosis, and now, though relieved to have the right answers, I found myself smack-dab in the middle of an identity crisis.

Who was I?
What did I really want my life to look like?
What new beliefs did I need to take hold of in order to get there?

Now, please hear me say this: I believe in the need for mental health care, medication, and accurate diagnoses. But I was disappointed in the doctors and psychiatrists who didn't keep digging to find the right answer for me. Mostly, I was frustrated with myself for allowing my beliefs to shift so much in that season. I became what I believed I had to be, and it turns out that was all wrong from the start.

If you aren't sure of your beliefs, you'll be unsure of just about everything else. You'll find yourself walking down paths you never thought you'd find yourself on, making choices you don't really want to make, and even becoming someone you don't really want to be. And it starts with what you allow yourself to believe. If you want to walk securely forward, you must start by building a foundation for your beliefs rooted in the truth of who you are and Whose you are.

In those years, it ultimately wasn't the wrong diagnosis or my reaction to it that led me so far away from who I was. It was the shaky beliefs I built my life on. The words my doctors said, the opinions of others, the fear that ruled my mind, the ruminating thoughts that etched my belief into stone—those were the things I built my belief system on. Those things wouldn't have lasted, diagnosis or not.

I decided to examine my beliefs then and there. To take stock and understand what was motivating me. To throw out what was not true and hold on to what was true. To build my identity from that point forward on the words of the God who made me, loves me, and wants what's best for me. To make the truth of Whose I am the foundation of my beliefs.

And that's what I want to challenge you to do, too! Before you can move forward with confidence in who you are, you have to make sure you believe the words of Whose you are. Why? Because God is the only unchanging, unconditional, unwavering place you can go in this world. If you want the pieces of what you believe to be built on steady ground, then you have to build them here. In a world where everything has the potential to change, to let you down, to deceive or disappoint you, God is the only place you can go to find stability, security, and unchanging truth. He is the only place on which you can build lasting beliefs.

Perhaps you need some help here. If so, consider the words of the very One who created you. Take time to hear God speak truth over who you are and Whose you are. Let these words become the foundation of your beliefs.

I am Jesus' friend. -John 15:14
I am a joint heir with Jesus, sharing His inheritance with Him. -Romans 8:17
I am united with God and one spirit with Him. -1 Corinthians 6:17
I am a member of Christ's body. -1 Corinthians 12:27
I am holy -Ephesians 1:1
I am free from condemnation. -Romans 8:1
I am a new creation because I am in Christ. -2 Corinthians 5:17
I am established, anointed, and sealed by God. -2 Corinthians 1:21
I do not have a spirit of fear, but of love, power, and a sound mind. -2 Timothy 1:7
I am not alone. -Matthew 28:20

Recently, I was speaking at a women's event where each person in the audience was handed a card with a truth from Scripture written on it. I prayed over the empty seats before the event as I always do, but this night, I specifically prayed that each woman would get the word and verse they most needed to believe.

This was just after my dad passed away, so I was especially nervous to be back on stage that night. In that message, I was going to talk about my dad, and my mom was coming to listen. I knew she needed encouragement, so I also prayed for the card she would receive. Do you know which one she was given entirely at random at the door?

"Not alone."

Perhaps you could call that coincidence, but I like to believe God speaks into your life when you are ready to hear Him. Everything about my mom's life had changed with my dad's passing. And God knew that her beliefs might shift with it. So, He spoke the truth that she needed to hold on to—the piece she needed to believe. She was, in fact, not alone.

Unfortunately, you don't always have someone speaking these truths into your ears to help you believe them. You often don't find a reason to examine your beliefs at all. Instead, you live controlled and condemned by wrong beliefs without even realizing it. And when that happens, you're missing out on believing the truth of who you are from the words of Whose you are. Even worse, when you operate with the wrong belief, it takes you to the wrong destination. And because I want you to get to the right destination for your life, I'd like to challenge you to consider your beliefs with me.

1. Examine your beliefs.

Let's start here! Because you can't build our beliefs on the right things if you don't even know what those beliefs are. So, begin by asking yourself what absolute truths you hold in your mind. What do you know for sure? What motivates your thoughts, choices, and behaviors? Where did those things come from? Your mind, your experiences, the words of someone else? In short, I'm asking you to think about what you believe and why you believe it.

When I was younger, my dad did this exercise with me often. Whenever I gained a new opinion (often about things like taxes or who should be ordained … you know, worldly decisions that I thought I had conquered in my teenage experience), he would sit me down and ask me to explain it. His goal wasn't to convince me of anything as absolute; instead, it was to subtly give me space to explore what I believed and why I believed it. It was a simple conversation with my dad at the time, but now I see this powerful exercise as an invaluable tool for defining my belief system. It required me to question my beliefs and understand why I had them in the first place. That's what I want you to be able to do, too!

2. Be honest about what your beliefs are motivating you to think or do.

Let me be real with you here. This one is going to require a *lot* of self-awareness and humility. It will require you to think about your choices, thoughts, and behaviors—to examine them for the good and the bad they've brought into your life. It will require you to get real with yourself about what led you to where you are now. It will require you to consider what beliefs may push you forward to places you don't want to be.

Sounds fun, right?

I know from experience this is hard. But I also know the best stuff in life often comes from the hard work it takes to get there. Defining your beliefs is no exception. When I discussed this with my Kaleidoscopes, they shared so much wisdom that came from examining their motivations in the shadow of their beliefs.

One Kaleidoscope has long endured Vitiligo, a condition that changes your skin tone. She waited and yearned for relief from her "spots" because she believed it would make her feel more self-confident. Now, a new drug is available to treat Vitiligo effectively, and she's questioning if she really needs it. Why? Because she's done the work. She's spent time in prayer, counseling, and more examining why she believed this condition made her "less than." Then, she looked at how it motivated her to hide or cover up. When she did the work of examining how that belief was causing her to act, she was able to make a shift. So much so that she wasn't sure she even wanted to change anymore. Her new belief became clear: She could be comfortable in her own skin.

You have to look at your beliefs and know how they drive your behavior. If you want to change the destination you are driving toward, you have to be willing to be honest about how your beliefs have led you there.

3. Lean into the true beliefs.

You might ask if it is healthy or beneficial, but this can be a tricky question to answer. Sometimes, what feels beneficial at the moment is not true. Even if it hurts, what is true will lead you where you need to be instead of where you are.

I don't always like what the scale tells me when I check my weight, but it doesn't mean it's untrue. I don't love what the bloodwork reveals about my cholesterol, but it is my responsibility to find the truth and act on it. I don't enjoy disagreeing with my husband, but deep down, I know I need to honor his viewpoint.

Could I hold on to the beliefs that make me feel better all the time? Sure! But would those things be true? Would they be healthy and helpful to me? Not in the long run. So why not anchor our beliefs in the places that are true? Even if those places are painful or hard to face, they'll ultimately serve us better.

One of my Kaleidoscopes believed that drinking was a safe way to numb the pain of her brother's death. By outside appearances, she was holding down a job, volunteering at school, and even running long distances to stay in shape. She was able to pass it off as a drink with friends or at dinner, but over time, one drink turned into many. And eventually, it consumed her.

Soon, she was struggling, not just with the drinking but with the beliefs she had around it. She believed she was in control, but she wasn't. She believed this was only a season, but it wasn't. She believed she could never admit to her job or children that she needed help, but she had to.

So, with the support of her husband and kids, she made a hard choice to go to rehab and deal with it. She chose to stop believing what wasn't true and embrace new beliefs that would serve her better in the long run.

So, how do you know if a belief is true? Start by asking yourself a few questions:

Is this in line with God's Word?
Is something about this belief making me anxious?
Why am I having trouble accepting this belief?
Would acting on this belief make my life better or worse?

Assess the beliefs you're holding on to from that lens. Start by getting real about your beliefs that may not be true, healthy, or helpful. Then, consider where you can go from there.

4. Pay attention to the tension.

When it comes to a belief, where do you feel tension? Paying attention to tension is essential as it can tell us one of two things. The first, I talked about above. Perhaps the belief is causing tension because it's not helpful or healthy for you. Maybe you aren't being honest with yourself about what it means.

The second can be equally as true. Maybe the belief is causing tension because it's time to let it go. It's a belief that's no longer serving you. It's a belief that maybe even wasn't yours to hold on to in the first place. If that's the root of the tension, then it's time to let it go.

Of course, I've had to let go of my fair share of beliefs along the way. Most recently, I had to drop the belief holding me back from the very work you're holding—the belief I could never write a book.

Once, I worked up the courage to ask a friend who had published a book to read a draft of something I was working on privately for teenagers overcoming hardships. I asked him for feedback and sincerely appreciated his willingness to give it. It took him several weeks to respond, but when he did, his honesty stung.

"I don't know how to tell you this, but the book is not very good."

Though he offered helpful critiques after that, I was stuck on that sentence alone. I took his word for it, tucked the book away in a drawer, and never showed it to another person. I let his words become a belief and held on to it for nearly a decade.

It wasn't until I was sitting in a meeting with the students at Lydia's Place that I realized what I was believing and how it was holding me back. I shared this example with the students, telling them how I'd never be able to write a book. One of the students quipped, "Miss April, do you find it strange that you tell us that we can do anything, but you don't think you can write a book?"

She was so right. The beliefs I'd bought into were holding me back. So, I had to let them go if I wanted to go forward. I had to lean into the tension to see that it was stopping me in my tracks. And well, here I am!

Your beliefs are powerful pieces. They influence so much about not just who you are and Whose you are, but where you go, what you do, and who you become in this life. So, you must be willing to examine those beliefs. Will it be easy? Oh, not at all! But the clarity, beauty, and abundance that comes on the other side? They're worth it.

If I've learned one thing from examining my beliefs over the years, it's this: True beliefs won't crumble under the weight of examination.

Instead, they'll stand.

Who You Are

- What is one belief you once held and now realize was false?
- What have you heard from other people in your life that shaped what you believe about yourself? Do they deserve a vote in your beliefs?
- What beliefs currently drive your behavior? Are you happy with the way they're leading you?
- Are there beliefs that you need to let go of?

Whose You Are

- Do you spend more time/energy focused on what God thinks about you or what you believe about yourself?
- Did the beliefs that are most important to you come from culture or God's Word?
- How has God's Word informed your belief system?
- What might change about your life if your beliefs were rooted in the truth of Whose you are?

A Prayer

Dear God,

I know I believe in You. My beliefs get tangled up, so I need You to unravel the beliefs that take my focus away from You. I know that my mind is limited. Help me discover Your truth about the things that I believe. Give me the humility I need to be open to Your truth. I pray for the courage to examine my beliefs and root them in your Word. Change my heart to focus on Your truth.

Help me look through the lens of Your love and trust that You worked out all the details in my life to point me to You. I pray You are shaping who I am. Mold me into who You want me to be and help me reflect Your love to the world.

Take all of my pieces and use them to point others to You.

Amen.

A Truth to Remember

To the Jews who had believed him, Jesus said, "If you hold to my teaching, you are really my disciples. Then you will know the truth, and the truth will set you free" (John 8:31-32 NIV).

CHAPTER SIX

The Rule Piece

My dad traveled a lot when my brother and I were small children, so he let my mom call the shots on most of the day-to-day parenting. Together, they raised us with much love but not many rules. We had a big pantry full of yummy snacks but very few rules about when or what we could eat. Everyone loved to play at our house because my mom devised creative ways to have fun and didn't mind the mess. She would buy minnows and small nets to fill up a cement pond in our backyard and let all the neighborhood kids come for fishing and popsicles. Once, when she was replacing a chandelier, she gave me the pieces to make crystal jewelry, and then she wore them to church at Christmas every year after. We had every pet imaginable and got to play with them all in the house. Long before Pinterest, my mom hosted theme birthday parties—not cute or perfectly done, but totally creative. I once had a hat party where we made hats from paper plates before putting on a parade. She let me put on Christmas pageants with the neighborhood kids and host random events at our house with very little notice or planning.

Rules, as I said, were limited.

Maybe we didn't need a lot of rules because my mom always knew where we were and what we were doing. Just before my senior trip in high school, I decided I wanted to get my belly button pierced. You had to be eighteen to do it, and my birthday was about a week too late. So, I convinced a friend to pierce my belly button with an ear-piercing gun. (This is something I do not recommend.) I thought I made the perfect plan to pull it off. I didn't ask for permission; I just did it.

You know, moms figure out everything. Of course, the morning after, I woke up very sore. Mom jumped in the bed with me, put her arm right on my belly, and when I flinched, she said coyly, "Oh, is something wrong?" Limited rules didn't mean I was excused from consequences (self-inflicted, in this case).

That's the thing about rules: I think something in us wants to push against them. It's been my experience that when you show someone a rule, they'll often test how close to the edge they can push it.

You can look no further than Adam and Eve to see how tempting it is to push against the rules. But let's be honest: You don't have to go back centuries to know that's true. You can probably go back a week, a day, an hour, a moment to think about the last time you tested a rule and had to live with the consequences.

Do I think some of this is in our nature as humans? Absolutely! But I also think this pushback comes from being hit with rules in every area of our lives. We're surrounded by a lengthy list of dos and don'ts that can make keeping up with every one of them nearly impossible.

Think about the rules you may have been given at home growing up.

Eat what's on your plate.
Make your bed and clean your room.
Homework before fun.
Be nice to your siblings.
Say "please" and "thank you."
Dress appropriately when you leave the house.

And what about the rules that come with dating and relationships?

Agree to a date, even if you don't want to, so you don't hurt anyone's feelings.
No kissing on the first date.
Hold your social media horses, and don't define the relationship too fast.
Go to coffee first, so you aren't committed to a whole meal if you don't like them.

Or consider the cultural rules adopted by your context or community.

No wearing white after Labor Day.
Tipping is not a suggestion; it is an expectation.
It's rude to be late.
Make eye contact when someone is talking to you.

As a Southern girl, I can't help but take this opportunity to highlight a few of my region's many rules here.

Sit like a lady.
Say "yes ma'am" and "no sir."
Always offer refreshments to guests.
Take off your hat at the dinner table.
Send a thank you note (not a text or email) for a gift.

And what about the rules in the workplace?

Answer the phone by the third ring.
Never discuss compensation.
Turn your camera on for Zoom calls.
Work hard, but don't take credit.

And maybe, the hardest of all, the rules that come from church or religion.

Women aren't allowed in leadership.
You have to be a member to be baptized.
There's a right way to pray.
Be in the church every time the doors are open.
Raise your hands in the contemporary service, but sing quietly in the traditional service.

There are family codes of conduct you may not even be aware you're following.

Do you talk about politics or not?
Do you consume alcohol in your homes?
Do you address conflict or brush it under the rug?
Do you spend all the holidays together?
And then, of course, there are the rules you have for yourself.
I'm going to exercise every single day.
I will limit my time on social media each day.
No alcohol except on the weekends.
I'll dress well anytime I leave the house.
I'm always going to apologize when I'm wrong.
I'll get my kids to school on time every day.

It's a lengthy list, right? There are written rules, and there are unwritten rules. Look back at this list and see which apply to you. Which ones do you see in your life, your family, your workplace, your faith? Which rules make you cringe? What rules would you add to the list?

No matter where they come from or which ones make our list, we're piled up with so many dos and don'ts that we're surrounded by rules at every turn. On the surface, that's not a bad thing. People need rules to keep them safe, help them function, and point them toward what's best. The hard part comes when those rules push against one another. When they conflict, how are we supposed to know what's good? What's right? And most importantly, what honors God?

I've seen this conflict play out often since Maria joined our family. Maria often tells us about cultural codes or rules from her family, community, or church in Nigeria. When she came to live with us, Maria could not wear pants, makeup, necklaces, nail polish, or relax her hair. When she arrived, I made a bag of new things I thought would help her settle. Little did I know, the rules she held herself accountable to prevented her from even opening it. Maria has since taught me so many other rules her culture placed on her, specifically as a woman, that differ from the ones she's found in America. For example, she thought it wrong to be with a man after dark, and if she were even to go to lunch with a man and then not marry him, it would disgrace her family. And, when it comes to dating, there is no kissing until the wedding day.

When I delved into this with Maria, I got overwhelmed by all the rules. And yet, Maria has been fascinated with some of our rules similarly: Traffic rules, time awareness rules, and even rules for how we greet each other, which conflict with her upbringing. Let's be honest here: Maria landed in the South, so she has been met with a whole host of rules that are even harder for me to explain. Imagine her expression when I explained to her that people here say they're "fine" when they really aren't!

That begs the question: How do we know which ones matter if we're constantly given rules to follow? Who's making the rules? And how do we know whose rules are right for us?

For me, there is a clear answer: God's rules are the rules that matter. If I believe who I am is shaped by Whose I am, shouldn't I abide by the rules given to me by the One who made me? Again, in theory, that's a simple answer: YES! But in reality, it's a bit more complex.

When Kip and I decided to get married, I felt a lot of angst about wearing a white dress. Why? Because this was my second wedding. I'd been married before, and I thought that meant, by God's standards, I wasn't pure enough to wear white on my wedding day. When I mentioned this to a friend and pastor, he was stunned.

"April, have you ever met a guy who said, 'I have been married before, so I can't wear a tuxedo to my wedding?'" he asked.

I shook my head in reply.

"Show me in the Bible where it says you can only wear white on your wedding day if you have never been married before," he challenged.

Of course, I couldn't do it because the Bible has nothing to say about wearing white to your wedding! Mary Queen of Scots was the first to wear a white wedding dress, and then Queen Victoria began the tradition by wearing a white dress to her wedding in 1840, which is when it became a symbol of purity. I was operating by rules I thought were given to me by God but were not His doing at all. This prompted me to evaluate the rules in my life with a new standard.

For me, now the question is simply this: "Is this a God rule?"

It's a question I think you should all be asking yourself. Because if you want to live in the fullness of who you are, you must listen to the leading—to the rules—of Whose you are. And to do that, you have to redefine how you see those rules.

So often, when discussing rules, they are shone in a negative light. They're there to hold us back, keep us from having fun, or force us to stay inside some imaginary lines. Honestly, sometimes it feels that way, but there's a difference in God's rules that sets them apart.

And that difference is love.

God's boundaries are in place for your good and His glory. They're pieces of a bigger story that lead to both. The purpose of God's rules is to guide you in how to love God, love yourself, and love others. They aren't rules made to be broken; they're rules made to heal. His rules show you the path of life. They show you who you are made to be.

Everything changes when you approach God's rules with that under-standing—the understanding they're built on love.

Then, they're not restrictive; they're rewarding.
They're not killing joy; they're bringing delight.
They're not holding us back; they're making us safe and secure.
They're not hurting; they're helping.
They're not keeping us captive; they're setting us free.

Growing up, my dad repeatedly told me about a study done on school playgrounds. Researchers made an interesting discovery about how children play, depending on whether there is a fence around the playground. If the playground had a fence around it, the kids would play in the entire space. But with no fence, the children played much closer to the playground equipment rather than exploring the schoolyard with as much freedom.

And so, it goes with us, God's children. Rules are not a bad thing. In fact, boundaries are most often a great thing because they allow us to live more freely. I think God loves us so much that He gave us rules to help us avoid living with consequences. When we stray from those rules, it doesn't mean God loves us less. It simply means we hurt more. I think my parents gave a snapshot of this in their parenting style. They were more interested in who I was becoming than the rules they wanted me to follow, and I think God is the same! He isn't holding us to a standard of rules simply to torture or teach us. He wants the very best for us—that's the outcome He desires. And the rules, or standards, He gives us to live by help us get there.

Piece by piece, they help you to be free.
Free to be who you are because of Whose you are.

So, how do you get there? How do you embrace the best set of rules from Whose you are so that you can walk forward knowing who you are?

1. Evaluate the rules you're following.

Think about the primary rules you have for yourself. I'm not talking about the laws citizens must obey. Those are unavoidable things you have to follow. I'm talking about the personal rules or standards you choose to live by regularly.

Ask yourself:

Where did that rule come from?
What is it leading me to think, do, or believe?
Is it in line with who I am?
And is it from Whose I am?

If the rules are rooted in the truth of who you are because of Whose you are, hold to them. But if they aren't? Well, I think it's time to re-evaluate.

I experienced this as a mom while preparing Lydia for her fourth birthday party. Just before the guests arrived, we reviewed some things to remember. In other words, I wanted to give her my list of unwritten rules for being gracious hosts. I reminded her to make sure all her friends were included, respect the adults in the room, and express gratitude for the gifts she received. Finally, I told her, "Just be sure to act like you like every single gift you receive, even if you don't."

In my mind, this was a rule we followed to be polite, but to my four-year-old daughter, it was outrageous.

"Mommy, isn't that telling a lie?" she pushed back.

Yes, Lydia, it is. Her seemingly simple question showed me that it was time to re-evaluate that rule or at least how I was teaching it.

2. There will be consequences.

Listen, you aren't going to get this right all the time. No matter how rooted in God your rules are, you will inevitably break them. You're going to misstep and mess up along the way. And because of that, you will face the consequences from time to time. Just because God loves you doesn't mean He frees you from consequence. If you want to hear His comforting voice, you can expect to hear His convicting voice, which often happens when you want to hear it the least. I think it's because of God's love that He allows you to experience the consequences. Breaking the rules (often called "sin" in religious spaces) separates you from God. It also usually makes you feel downright awful. Still, you have to learn the lesson, which sometimes means learning it the hard way.

One of my students once shared a story about a pesky rooster. He would harass the rooster and then run to tell his dad when the rooster finally pecked him. His dad asked, "Well, did you pick on the rooster?"

"No, Daddy!" he replied.

This entire exchange happened three times over several days. Each time, his dad questioned if he had followed and respected the rooster's boundaries and each time, the boy assured him he had. Finally, after the third time he came to complain, his dad took action. He asked the boy to follow him outside, where he killed the rooster right in front of him.

Harsh? Yes! Memorable? Absolutely!

My student recalled crying as his dad said, "Why are you crying? If you didn't bother this rooster, it attacked you for no reason."

At this, he shrugged a little, admitting finally that he may have not been as innocent in harassing the dearly departed rooster as he'd led his father to believe.

"Well, what can you learn from this?" his dad asked.

"Not to mess with the rooster," he muttered through tears.

"Well, yes, but more importantly, son, you have to know the consequences."

3. There will also be grace.

The bad news? You're always going to be rule-breakers in some form or fashion. It's part of being human. You can't get it right all the time. But the good news? God gives you grace to get you through. So yes, there will be consequences, but there will always be grace.

As a teenager, I broke one of my own rules. I had such guilt that I scheduled a lunch with my pastor to tell him. I realized this was not typical, but for the most part, I was a rule follower. His response surprised me.

"Have you told your parents?" he asked.

"Not yet," I responded.

"What do you think they will say?"

Looking back, I think he asked the question because he knew them well enough to know their response. He knew they would extend grace. And to be honest, so did I.

"I think they'll tell me they love me. They will say they're concerned, but they love me," I finally answered.

He nodded his agreement before adding, "I think that's what God would say, too."

I skip telling you my specific mistake here to allow you to fill in your own. Like I said, you're bound to mess up and make mistakes. Left to yourself, you can't keep all the rules. Not perfectly or completely, and not all the time. And while that does mean you're bound to face the consequences at some point or another, it also means you get to experience God's grace amid those mess-ups.

And that's a gift! Because, in the absence of grace, most often find self-destruction. The way people beat themselves up over following invisible rules can be extreme. Before they know it, they're consumed with thoughts like …

I am failing miserably.
People will think I don't have it together.
They will think I am stupid.
I will be judged.

Friend, let me remind you that these thoughts are not from God. And when you experience them, it is important to gaze into the grace of Whose you Are.

4. Boundaries are for your benefit.

Yes, some rules and laws are universal. Again, those aren't the standards I'm talking about here. I'm talking about the rules you set for yourself. The rules you put in place for your own accountability and protection. Boundaries that help you protect what is important.

Take the example of one of my Kaleidoscopes. As a stay-at-home mom, she was always running around and filling her free time, helping other moms with their tasks and to-do lists. That's just the kind of person she is! But eventually, she wore herself out and had to set a new rule for herself: She'd take care of herself first. It was a shift in how she'd operated—a new rule or boundary to set her free. When she felt rested and cared for, she would make more space for others. But until then, she had to take care of herself and her family first. She knew what she needed and had to write new rules to get there. Those new rules? They gave her a standard to help her experience more freedom in her own life.

That's what rules can do! They're meant to set you free. Living by rules you have examined with God's Word permits you to set boundaries in line with who you are and Whose you are. Remember that you can be loving, considerate, and kind and still have boundaries. It gives you the authority to say yes or no confidently without looking back. I know this seems counterintuitive or hard to believe, but rules are a good thing. God's rules—not church rules, not cultural codes of conduct, not fictional rules in your head—are pieces designed for your good. You'll find comfort, joy, and peace when you approach rules from His love.

I pray you will find the courage to examine the rules that rule your life. As you do, hold them up and ask yourself, "Does this rule come from God? Does it honor both who I am and Whose I am?" If the answer is yes, keep going, friend. But if the answer is no, I pray you dare to re-evaluate, recommitting to God's rules and tossing out the ones that no longer belong to you and those around you.

Who You Are

- How do you decide which rules matter for you?
- Have you ever lived by a rule you later determined was not right for you?
- Think of a time you obeyed a rule, even when you didn't like or understand it. How did it help you avoid consequences?
- Define your boundaries. What are some rules you live by?

Whose You Are

- What rules do you think are overwhelming when you consider faith, either for yourself or someone considering becoming a follower of Jesus?
- What rules are the hardest to follow? What blessing is on the other side of those rules?
- Is there a rule you've broken that makes it hard to believe you could receive forgiveness? Can you conceive of God's capacity to forgive and allow you to begin again?
- Are there rules you don't understand that are a part of the church culture?
- How does following God's rules make you different from other people? Why do you suppose God asks this of you?

A Prayer

Dear God,

Thank You for giving us rules. Give me the grace to see Your rules through the lens of Your love and to trust that they are divine—a blessing created for my protection. Show me which rules matter. Help me to know and obey Your rules and give me the courage to reject those not Yours. Break my walls down. Flood Your love over me for the rules I have broken and the unrealistic expectations I have given myself. Help me extend this same grace to other people as well.

Help me look through the lens of Your love and trust that the rules You have given me help me live more closely with You. I pray You are shaping who I am. Mold me into who You want me to be and help me reflect Your love to the world.

Take all my pieces and use them to point others to You.

Amen.

A Truth to Remember

In fact, this is love for God: to keep his commands. And his commands are not burdensome, for everyone who is born of God overcomes the world. This is the victory that has overcome the world, even our faith (1 John 5:3-4 NIV).

CHAPTER SEVEN
The Piece You Value

Somewhere around the time our youngest, Anne Marie, turned four, I decided I wanted to revamp my wardrobe. It was our tenth wedding anniversary, and Kip and I were going on a trip for our first extended time away since having two babies. To get ready, I asked my friends Katrina and Lindsay to help me get some outfits together.

I can't even describe the embarrassment of the fashion show that crawled out of my closet.

My friends giggled over the hats, belts, and wardrobe staples in my closet that were ... well, bad. I'm talking tons of stuff that was likely never in style, even when I purchased it. Still, they helped me put together a few presentable outfits. I took pictures on my phone to avoid forgetting what we'd picked out. I clearly couldn't be trusted left to my own style devices.

After a few hours of their time, side-splitting laughs, and several outfits, my friends gave me something valuable that day. First, they were honest with me. Their statements like, "That is not your best look," or, "That does not look like you," helped. But perhaps even more important, my friends encouraged me to speak up when I saw something I didn't like. So, when they'd present me with an item of clothing from my closet—an item I bought! —that didn't feel right, I'd exclaim, "NOT THAT!" It sounds silly, but it was an amazing gift. The encouragement to define what I didn't like helped me figure out what I did like. It helped me define what was important to me in my wardrobe.

It helped me learn how to articulate what I valued.

That's something I needed to learn beyond my wardrobe. It's something we all need to learn how to do. Because when it comes to identity, your values play a more prominent role than you may realize.

Before I go on, let's distinguish values from other things I've discussed. Remember, beliefs are what a person holds to be real and true. Rules are the code of conduct that people use to carry out those beliefs. Values help people decide what is right or wrong. They help determine what goals to strive for and what personal qualities to develop. In short, values are things that you deem important. They're standards for discerning what is best. They're pieces deeply embedded and critical in determining who and what is most important.

I'd argue that your values become most apparent when you look at the things you spend your time and money on, what you like, who you're drawn to, what decisions you make, and the like. If you value honesty, you will likely trust the more honest people in your life. If you value hard work, you will spend a lot of time showing it's true to your boss, coworkers, and even yourself. If you value equality, you will spend time fighting for it and surround yourself with people who do the same.

In the same way, if a value is important to you, you will likely notice its absence in others. If you value compassion, you will distance yourself from people who don't show it to others. If you value kindness, you will have little time for those who lead with unkindness. And if you value freedom, you will limit your time with people or things that threaten your feeling of freedom.

What's interesting about values is that they're the same wherever you go. Most people don't have one set of values for friends and another for family. They don't operate with one set of values in marriage and another in parenting. They don't display one set of values at church and another at work. They don't have Saturday night values and Sunday morning values (or at least they shouldn't!). Because when someone really knows their values—if they're strong and rooted in the right place—they won't shift from person to person or circumstance to circumstance.

Your values should remain steady in any situation because you know them, just as assuredly as you know who you are and Whose you are.

If you're like me and enjoy checking off boxes, it's important to remember that values are not goals. They shouldn't be a reflection of who you want to be or what you hope to hold important; they're pieces of who you are that impact how you make decisions day to day.

For example, I want to be the mom who has dinner on the table for my family every night so we can sit together and talk about our day. But no matter how much I want that to be true of who I am, it just isn't. I hate to cook, and we have activities almost every night of the week. So, I had to shift my focus to the value rather than the activity. Rather than try to be the mom who cooks every night for her family,

I became the mom who was present for her kids and found other ways to spend quality time as a family. Ultimately, the food on the table wasn't what I valued; it was the time with my family.

I could apply this principle to almost any part of my life.

I want to be the athletic, organized, patient, calm, adventurous, world-traveling Pinterest mom who only serves organic food and volunteers at the school all the time.

I want to serve at a thriving non-profit where I can be present, be prepared for every meeting, be available to answer my phone anytime someone calls with a need, be dressed for the part, push for excellence, support our team, and be respected in the community.

I want to have our cute little hobby farm in neat order and spend time with each animal.

And I want to grow my business with speaking engagements and new coaching opportunities.

But the truth is, I can't be all of that.

And neither can you.

You can only be you. And, when you define who you are, Whose you are, and what you really value because of that, there's a freedom to be found on the other side.

Take this list of common values to start. Of course, this is not an exhaustive list, so please add to it if you feel other words encompass your values. Take a moment to read through it, add any of your own, and then narrow it down to just your top four values.

Accountability	Family	Kindness
Commitment	Lifelong learning	Family
Harmony	Honesty	Authenticity
Discipline	Respect	Fairness
Adventure	Humor	Collaboration
Open-mindedness	Dependability	Excellence
Service	Achievement	Knowledge
Education	Truth	Curiosity
Courage	Competition	Creativity
Love	Legacy	Persistence
Fun	Friendship	Quality
Faith	Equality	Health
Simplicity	Independence	Structure
Balance	Change	Recognition
Influence	Order	Empathy
Beauty	Teamwork	Challenge
Efficiency	Initiative	Communication
Happiness	Honor	Integrity
Loyalty	Innovation	Community
Freedom	Hard work	Diversity
Self-control	Patience	Risk-taking
Fitness	Comfort	Congruency
Significance	Reverence	Adaptability
Hope	Reliability	Vulnerability
Understanding	Uniqueness	Generosity
Making a difference	Personal growth	Forgiveness
Contribution	Power	Compassion
Gratitude	Sustainability	Trust
Leadership	Belonging	Travel

Thrift	*Empowerment*	*Success*
Inclusion	*Independence*	*Intuition*
Joy	*Passion*	*Tradition*
Vision	*Wisdom*	

Knowing your values can help you understand who you are. It gives clarity to hold on to in times of challenge and uncertainty. It can help you make intentional decisions that not only reflect what you hold dear—what you value—but also the core pieces of your identity, who you are and Whose you are.

I remember the night my first marriage ended. It had been over for a long time, but, at the time, I naively thought divorce was for people who didn't try hard enough. So, I committed to two years of counseling to make it work. Our counselor asked us individually to write down our "absolutes" on a piece of paper. In other words, she was asking us to name our values. So, we did. And friend, nothing we wrote down aligned. None of our absolutes were absolute for each other. With that reality finally on paper, our counselor said definitively, "I really think we are finished here."

The following morning, I loaded everything I could fit in my car. I was teaching a class that night, so I spent the drive there mentally preparing myself to put on a smile. On the bright side, I had become a master at faking it. So, that night, I faked my way through class. Yet, unlike other nights spent teaching, I fell to my knees and wept when the last student left the room.

Lost,
alone,
desperate,
and very, very sad.

This was obviously not what I had imagined.

I'd never been more stressed or worried, and do you want to know the title of the lesson I taught that night? "How to Stop Worrying and Start Living." On top of that, I was brought up in a home that looked a lot like *Leave it to Beaver*. My parents loved each other, and they loved me. I checked all the boxes on paper and tried to change myself to make the marriage work. So, just what was I doing on the proverbial floor? What was I doing in a ball of anger and angst? How did I get there? How did I lose sight of who I was and what I valued? And how would I find both again?

A year later, I was still lost. So, I signed up for a divorce care class at church. Kara, a friend I met in class, sat across from me one night when asked to partner up for a seemingly simple activity: We were supposed to think about things that brought us joy.

"I like spaghetti," she said.
"I like country music," I said.

And on and on, we went back and forth as we named more and more things we loved. The shocking part for Kara and I was how much we'd forgotten what we liked. We didn't know what our preferences were, much less our values. We had lost so much of who we really were.

Later, the class gave us an assignment to set aside a day and make absolutely no plans, meaning a clear calendar and clear expectations about what we would accomplish in those hours. I learned so much about myself that day that I would encourage you to try it. Because when you spend time alone, you're able to pay attention to what you read or watch, what you see when you scroll, what you do with your money, where you put your time, and more. Do you follow a routine or like to have free time with no plans? Do you like to stay home or go out? Do you prefer to be with people or spend time by yourself? They're simple things but can help point you to what you value.

Why does this matter? At the end of the day, your values are integral pieces of who you are. They reflect your character and integrity in the world. Your character and integrity are on the line every day because when you give up a little bit of either, you lose a piece of who you are. If you aren't operating with a solid, strong value system—something you know to be true in any season or circumstance—you risk so much more than ending up somewhere you didn't intend to be. You risk losing who you really are.

As Andre Lorde puts it, "If I don't define myself for myself, I will be crunched into other people's fantasies for me and eaten alive." If you don't define your values, someone else will. It may be culture, relationships, social media, or even work. No matter what it is, the truth remains: If you don't decide your values, you leave room for someone else to decide for you.

So, what do you do? How do you walk forward with strong values rooted in the right things? Built out of who you are and Whose you are?

1. Remember, your value is found in Him.

I genuinely believe that you can't correctly determine what you value if you don't first understand how much God values you. Your values must be formed by the God who formed you. For me, this has become a foundational truth. I can't determine what I value without first resting on the value God has given me. Starting there gives me a firm, confident foundation to build on. My faith in God helps me know that my life has value. And then it helps me redefine what I value.

I want this to be true of you, too. I want you to know for certain just how much value you have in Christ. He planned for you. He designed you. He created every part of who you are. That fact alone gives you value. It gives you a sense of who you are that nobody can shake. To think that people have the power to define you is to deny the value Christ has already given you.

If you're unsure how God feels about you, look at Jesus. Everything He did and said—every interaction He had with God's people— shows us our value in Him. Jesus didn't eat with sinners and tax collectors because He wanted to appear inclusive, tolerant, and accepting. He ate with them because He loved them. He valued them, not for what they did or didn't do, but for who they were. Or more, for Whose they were. And the same is true for us!

So, before you can begin to know your values, you have to know your value. You have to know who you are is defined by Whose you are. Then, let the One who created you shape your values.

2. Define your values.

This is key. You can't operate from your values if you don't know what your values actually are. We did a quick exercise to name your values, but it's important you take time to give this more thought. Spend time over the next week paying attention to your behavior and asking additional questions to help you define your values.

What do you think other people would say your values are?

Where do you spend most of your money? Time? Energy?
What do you prioritize?
What guides your major decisions?
What matters most to you?
What bothers you? And what makes you do something about it?

Evaluate your values against your actions. For example, if your number one value is fun, can you name what you do for fun? If it is family, does that influence how you spend your time and energy? If it's trust, how are you demonstrating that in your day-to-day life?

Defining your values helps set your path toward the person you want to become. It gives you a lens through which to make major decisions and evaluate your priorities. Knowing your values helps you articulate what is important, allowing you the freedom to create boundaries. Clearly defined values give you the confidence and comfort to say no. In turn, you can fill your cup and stay focused. It allows you to prioritize, plan, and, most of all, protect what is most important. When your values are clearly defined, you have a strong foundation that acts as a compass, guiding your actions, decisions, and future.

I used to feel like I had all these pieces of my life that didn't make sense. Half of my friends saw my casual leggings and ponytail during morning drop-off and thought I was a stay-at-home mom because my schedule was so flexible for playdates. Another set of work friends saw me as a speaker and coach and only saw me in a suit. Still others saw me working for a non-profit, helping others and raising funds. Before, having such a split image would've thrown me for a loop. But now, because I can define empowerment as one of my top values, I know each aspect of my life aligns with what I value.

I want to empower my family, so I support my kids in school and activities and prioritize time with my husband. I want to empower the people I meet through speaking and training, so I work hard to provide value and do more than is expected. I want to empower my community and the students of Lydia's Place, so I give my time and energy to serving as a volunteer.

No matter how others see me or in what sphere I'm in, I know who I am. I know what's important to me. Keeping my eyes on that has helped me as a parent, a professional, and a non-profit founder. It's helped keep my focus on what matters most to me.

3. Avoid the drift.

Once you've defined your values, operating in spheres that encourage you to hold on to them is vital. Because the minute you lower your guard, you risk drifting from what you hold valuable. You risk losing sight of who you are and Whose you are. Just as a boat can gradually drift off course—so slowly you don't even realize it—you can drift off course from your values and not even realize it.

Founded in 1636, Harvard University initially only employed Christian professors. Their focus was on fulfilling the stated mission of instructing students to "know God and Jesus Christ."4 But today, from the outside, the school has no ties to its Christian roots. When I researched this further, I typed the following into the search: "Christian background and Harvard." The first article that populated was a question: "Can Christians attend Harvard?" They seem to have drifted from the values they started with, so much so that people aren't even aware it was a value in the first place.

---

4 https://www.thepublicdiscourse.com/2018/03/20951/

If we're not careful, the same can be true for us. I can value being present for my children and become distracted by other good things, even emails from their teachers or moms planning play dates. Suddenly, I'm spending the afternoon looking at my phone instead of spending focused time with my kids. Maybe you value your faith, but you pack your weekends so full you no longer have time to attend church. Maybe you're so busy serving others that you lose sight of the value of serving your family first.

Just like that, you've drifted.

What causes us to drift? It's not that you don't know what matters; maybe you just don't consistently evaluate your behaviors and choices through the lens of your values. Mission drift is like a slow drip. Over time, it happens, often without us even realizing it until it's too late.

Now, please here me say this: Values can shift and change with time. There's nothing inherently wrong with changing, growing, or adapting. The risk isn't in the change; it's in the drift. The drift happens when you don't intend to change, and that's where the danger lies.

It's important to note that you can be friends with and do life alongside people with differing values. This isn't a call to avoid anyone who may think differently than you. Your lives can be enriched by spending time with a diverse group of thinkers. But it is a call to be strong in your own values. Being confident of who you are and Whose you are and how those two things impact your value system allows you to do life with others whose values don't align with your own without the risk of drifting from what you hold important.

4. Listen to people who know your values.

A defined set of values speaks volumes about what matters to you and who you want to be. The more you live out of your values, the more others will know your values. And the benefit is that those closest to you can help point you back to what you value when you need it most.

During my season of personal repair after my marriage fell apart, I was admittedly more than a little lost. One night, I'd gone out with a bunch of girls for dinner before going to a bar with a small group. With some liquid courage, I quickly found myself on the dance floor. Of course, I thought I had great moves when in reality, it looked pretty tragic. On the dance floor, my friend Chris approached me, quietly grabbed my hand, and ushered me toward the door.

"We're going home, April," he said in a tone that conveyed both his kindness and his firmness.

So, home we went. When we got back to my apartment, Chris paused thoughtfully for a moment before he leaned in to share some much-needed truth with me.

"I don't know what has happened to you, my friend," he began, "but I need to remind you that this is not who you are."

Ouch!

Sure, it stung at the time, but now, I have to give Chris a lot of credit. He didn't just hold me accountable for what was fun or acceptable to him. He held me accountable for who he knew me to be. To my own character. To my own values.

Chris has done this for me multiple times, and it's a true gift. Because sometimes, it's easier for someone else to see you acting out of character than for you to recognize it in yourself. And when they see it—when they see you drifting from your values—they're the voices you need to pull you back to who you are.

5. Let your values guide key decisions.

Values are key in helping us walk the path designed specifically for you. Rather than holding your choices up to the world's standards, the opinions of others, or what you think you're supposed to do, your values can serve as the guiding force to lead you to exactly where you need to be. Values give you clarity. They help you make decisions and go your own route, even when that route is narrow.

When I had a six-month-old at home, I felt prompted to start Lydia's Place. Of course, I had absolutely no experience starting a non-profit and was in the throes of the baby stage, but I couldn't shake the feeling that this was the right thing for me to do. It felt like a sharp turn. I'd planned for years to have a career that would allow flexibility in my schedule and enough money to contribute to our household's finances. Starting a non-profit from the ground up would take both things off the table.

Of course, the people closest to me had questions.

Is this something you have to do right now?
Could you just volunteer somewhere else until you have more time?
Does this make sense financially?
Will this be good for your family?
Is this really what you want?

Were their questions valid? Of course! Were they trying to help me be sure I was making the right decision? Absolutely! Did their thoughts and feedback give me pause? They sure did!

I was sure of my values, and I felt sure I was being prompted to keep moving forward. But that didn't mean I wasn't hesitant to step out and actually do it. It took words of wisdom from my own child years later to remind me that I could trust my values to lead me.

During Vacation Bible School, Anne Marie was learning about the story of Jacob & Esau in Genesis. She eagerly listened to how Esau, who was hungry, went to his brother Jacob for food. In the middle of the lesson, Anne Marie raised her hand with a comment.

"Well, if someone is hungry, they just need to get my mommy's phone number because she has food and helps them," she explained with confidence.

Out of the mouth of babes, right? At the time, I was taking food to a student that my budding non-profit served. Truthfully, I was struggling with some mom guilt for leaving my girls at VBS without me there to volunteer. Admittedly, I was measuring myself against the moms who did stay. But can I tell you that all my guilt over not being with them at VBS that day dwindled as soon as I heard what Anne Marie said? Because my daughter knew what I valued and was proud of it. She saw me following the lead of my values to do the right thing. She understood it, and she helped me remember it, too.

When unsure if you're making the best choice, pause and think. Does the choice you're making help you follow the lead of your values? If it is, keep walking, friend. You can trust you're moving in the right direction, walking down the path toward who you are, thanks to Whose you are.

So, remember this: You have a unique set of values. Your values help you be your best self. And, when you root those values in Whose you are, they help shape every piece of your life, including who you are.

Your values help you set the standard for the person you truly are.

The person you were made to be.

Who You Are

- Reflect on a moment in your life when you felt clarity about something that was important to you. How did that show you what you value?
- Have you ever had a "not that" moment when you realized you were behaving in a way that didn't represent your values?
- What values do you see in other people that you respect, even if they are different than your own?
- How does your life and work currently reflect your values?
- Which of your top values are you ignoring or not giving enough attention to?

Whose You Are

- In what ways do your values align with God's Word? In what ways might they differ?
- How does defining your values help you give grace and love to others?
- How might focusing on Whose you are impact your values?

A Prayer

Dear God,

Thank You for knowing my name and, more importantly, my heart. Thank You that what is important to me is important to You. I want my values to reflect what You value. I want to lean into Your truth to determine what is most important to me. Guide me. Clarify my thoughts. Transform my mind and heart to have Your values. Help me to focus on what matters to You. Transform my values to align with Your values. I know Your Word says You will do this by renewing my mind. Help me to focus my life on what You value.

Help me look through the lens of Your love and have values that point other people to You. I pray You are shaping who I am. Mold me into who You want me to be and help me reflect Your love to the world.

Take all my pieces and use them to point others to You.

Amen.

A Truth to Remember

Pray for us. We are sure that we have a clear conscience and desire to live honorably in every way (Hebrews 13:18 NIV).

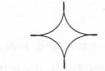

CHAPTER EIGHT
The Purpose Piece

When I was in seventh grade, I thought I discovered my purpose: I would change the world through recycling. I'd read a book on recycling and how it could benefit the environment. (Yes, I'm aging myself by admitting I'm old enough to remember when not everyone was recycling!). I believed I could do it. I was sure this change could start with me.

My plan was specific: I wanted to save enough money from the recycled items to pay for a pick-up service at our school and then get other schools to do the same. So, I set up bins and containers for people to drop their recyclable items all over my school. When my mom loaded up her big car with the results for the first time, the car was so full that there was hardly room for me to sit. But when it was all weighed, the total came out to a whopping twenty-three cents. It wasn't even enough to pay for the gas it took to get to the recycling plant! While money wasn't the motivation, it was a cold rush of reality. If an entire carload resulted in so little, how could I possibly change the world, one recycled piece of paper at a time?

Perhaps the most important thing that happened that day was my mom's reaction. She acknowledged that we didn't raise as much money as we wanted, but she also reminded me that we helped the environment with what we did. She encouraged me to keep thinking of ways to make my recycling idea work.

She encouraged me to keep pressing forward on what I felt was my purpose.

Sure, that whole program failed, but my desire to make a difference in the world didn't fade. Looking back on it, I think my mom's reaction that day had much to do with my belief that I could start a ministry to help foster youth. Even when a lot of people told me it was an uphill battle, even when it seemed impossible, even when it felt like I was carrying a car full of boxes and only making twenty-three cents, I kept going. I kept pursuing a purpose that my mom breathed life into all those years ago.

Ultimately, as a follower of Christ, my purpose is to know and serve God. Still, I often crave a way to carry this out in something tangible. For two decades now, I have listened to students' concerns and fears of being unimportant, old news, or irrelevant. Perhaps a greater fear should be being relevant where it doesn't matter.

Unfortunately, there is no definite way to magically find your purpose, but there are ways you can pay attention to help you focus. Take inventory of your strengths, relationships, and season of life. Pray and ask God for clarity. It will require some self-reflection, some honesty, and maybe even some change, but if purpose is an essential piece of who you are, then it's worth your attention.

So, I ask you …

What keeps you up at night with excitement?

What are you quietly enthusiastic about? What would you keep doing even if no one ever noticed?

How would you spend your time if you were financially secure and didn't need a salary?

What were some childhood interests you could never fully explore but still find interesting?

What do people tell you is your superpower? Your unique gift?

If you could pick three things to be remembered for after you pass, what would they be?

Is there someone whose life and work inspires and excites you? Who is it? Why?

What skills and or talents do you have that you are passionate about using?

What specific activities have you done that you enjoy and find engaging?

What are your values? What hints do they give you about your purpose?

How do you find fulfillment in your current day-to-day life?

What pain have you experienced that qualifies you to help others through personal experience?

Perhaps you have unique gifts that you enjoy sharing, like praying boldly, loving others when it's hard, celebrating small things, or giving generously. Maybe you have wisdom from your experiences or Biblical knowledge to pass on. Perhaps you are financially prudent and detail-oriented or great at building things. Maybe you love connecting people or teaching, serving, and helping others. You might be okay doing the same things over and over again and value structure or routine. You might be a leader everywhere you go, or you might be really good at following directions and doing what needs to be done behind the scenes. These aren't coincidences; these are all hints about your purpose!

Of course, it's important to remember that your purpose is unique to you. No answer is too big or too small because it's designed to fit just you. I saw this firsthand when I talked over the concept of purpose with my Kaleidoscopes.

Because one of my Kaleidoscopes loves making people happy and arranging flowers, she started a business to do just that, not to make money but to fill a place in her heart.

Another Kaleidoscope has spent decades studying the Bible. When I approached her about teaching me to study the Bible, she did not hesitate.

"This is my passion: getting other people excited about the Bible," she told me, adding just one caveat. "I'll spend whatever time you need, but if my children call during our meeting, I will take the call."

Yes, Suzanne is someone who knows her values and her purpose.

Another Kaleidoscope knows that her purpose is to help people get from where they are to where they want to be. I have seen her do this with countless women who feel lost or stuck as they re-enter the work world. For example, she helped her friend, Amy, who was questioning what to do once her kids started school. My friend looked at her resume and said, "You are a process improvement and start-up consultant." And today, that is precisely what Amy is doing.

Another Kaleidoscope was an atheist until her child shared the Gospel with her. In her own words, her purpose is now to help people come from darkness to light. She even wrote a book about the hard questions she had to overcome to believe so she might help others do the same.

These friends aren't waiting for purpose to find them. They're using their gifts, passions, and time, right here and right now. I think the same can be true for you.

But to get there, you must first be willing to put to rest any false ideas of purpose you may be holding onto. See, there is a shift that happens when you realize that, most often, your purpose is found right where you are. It doesn't have to be some big, grand, major platform purpose. It can simply be the role you're walking in each and every day.

Kip has helped me understand the importance of finding purpose in whatever role we are called to play. When people ask him what he does for a living, Kip consistently responds, "I work at Wal-Mart." The reaction varies from judgment and questions to statements about what a great company it is. The reality is that Kip used to think of his job as "just retail," but eventually, he realized that his purpose in the work was leading people. Leading people encompasses conversations about career paths and coaching, getting to know people, and encouraging and doing life with those he works alongside each day. He celebrates birthdays and attends funerals. He helps young adults plan for their future and gets to promote some of them. He learns their strengths, pushes them forward, and walks through the hard with them. Right where he is, Kip is living out his purpose.

And the best part? When you walk in our purpose, you help others begin to live out theirs. When you live out your purpose, it radiates to the people around you.

One of my Kaleidoscopes suffered severe anxiety and post-partum depression. Thankfully, she had a group of women rally around her to help her get through that tough season. Once she felt better, she looked around and realized she could see the same pain and hardship in other moms because of her experience. So, she made it her purpose to do something about it. She started a night of worship for women in her town, and now, the ministry has grown to have events in multiple communities and reach hundreds of women each year. By walking in her purpose, she has helped other women find the same freedom she did.

That's the thing about purpose! God will use you when you follow His lead and take the first step. Once you focus on your purpose, you will see that God, "who is able to do immeasurable more than all we ask or imagine, according to His power that is at work within us,"5 will open doors you never even thought possible. He will introduce you to people you would never have met. He will take the pieces of your purpose to do more than you can ask or imagine, just as promised.

God has a unique purpose just for you, so why not walk uniquely in it? So, as you begin exploring your purpose—the path designed for who you are by Whose you are—here are a few things to consider.

1. Explore your why.

This is a great place to start when it comes to purpose. It's important for you to determine what is driving you to do what you do. That's not only what will get you going; it's what will keep you going. If you don't know *why* you're doing what you're doing, you won't know *why* you need to press on when things get hard (and trust me, things will eventually get hard!).

---

5   Ephesians 3:20

Around the fourth year of Lydia's Place, I was struggling. We'd grown really fast (probably too fast!). With that growth, we also underwent some leadership changes, making the growing pains even more challenging. I had to step back in to lead more in that season; truth be told, it was hard.

I remember sitting in our office, wondering if it was time for us to close. Was this specific purpose coming to an end for me? The answer came very quickly when I considered visiting the kids living in our housing and telling them they no longer had a place to stay. Why was I doing this? For those kids! Remembering that helped me keep going.

So, figure out your why. Why do you do what you do? Keeping that in mind will help you better understand your purpose and stay encouraged to keep walking in it.

2. Focus on God's economy.

So often, people evaluate their sense of purpose by the world's standards. But this will only get you so far. If you believe your purpose is spoken into by Whose you are, you must evaluate your purpose by those standards. You must evaluate it through the lens of God's economy. You have to understand that God's measuring stick looks very different than the world's.

Your purpose does not have to be the world's biggest, best, or most notable purpose. It's unlikely that it will be. It's okay to realize that our purpose may seem small to others. So, ask yourself: How are you evaluating your purpose? Is it what the world deems as important? Or are you filtering it through God's calling for you?

Several years ago, I spoke at a women's event about this very topic. I shared about my work at Lydia's Place, hoping it would encourage the women. As I left the building after the talk, my friend walked over to me. She said, "That was awesome, and I am so proud of you. But I just feel like I'll never do anything that big. I mean, I just make peanut butter and jelly sandwiches every week."

Katy oversaw the donations from the women's group to Lydia's Place, and yes, she did make peanut butter and jelly sandwiches every week, but by the hundreds for children in our community who otherwise would not have lunch. And as I reminded her that morning, there is so much purpose in each of those sandwiches. Because purpose is not about doing something that puts you in the spotlight. It's about doing whatever you are called to do.

So, as you consider your own personal purpose, consider it through the lens of Whose you are. There, no purpose is too big or too small to make a mark.

3. Be flexible with the path, not the purpose.

There is a good chance you are going to hear "no." Sometimes it will be an all-out "NO!" Other times it will be a subtle, quiet response. Either way, it isn't easy when you experience hurdles. But remember, that hurdle—that no—could be re-direction toward a new path that will allow you to accomplish that same purpose.

When I felt called to start Lydia's Place, I started reaching out to people who worked in foster care. I told them about my dream to open a ranch for teenagers who were not likely to get adopted. Every single time, I was met with some version of a "no."

You're not going to be able to do that.
Laws are changing and won't support that kind of set up.
I don't know if you realize how much work that will be.

In short, I got a long list of reasons I could never make it work. It was a "no" everywhere I turned. I could've given up at that point. I could've decided God was closing the door. But the purpose was so clear in my heart I knew it wasn't over. So, I let the "no" do something different for me. I let it push me forward and help me find the courage to step out in faith in a new way.

When I envisioned Lydia's Place, I had big plans for a ranch-style environment with animals and a working farm. I dreamed of big houses full of parents who created a family with kids who had not found one of their own. Today, Lydia's Place is in a college town. We house our young adults in apartments, and they live independently rather than in a family environment. And you know what? It is working. We are serving kids and making an impact. The purpose is the same, but we carry it out differently than I envisioned.

You must be absolute in your purpose and flexible in how you carry it out. Trust me when I tell you there is power in the pivot when you are flexible with where God prompts and leads.

4. Find people who encourage you in your purpose.

One of the best things I've found in my life is the encouragement from friends and loved ones to keep walking my purpose. They are the voices that push me to keep going, keep growing, and keep my eyes on my purpose. And I believe that's invaluable to all of us looking to walk in purpose.

When you live among other people on purpose, you live as part of the body of Christ. Since God created each person uniquely, He can use your different strengths and interests. It's important to remember that He can use anyone who is willing.

When I volunteered as a coach to become a Dale Carnegie instructor, I often leaned on advice from my mom, who was also an instructor. I can remember calling her when I thought of quitting because the hours were long, and it seemed I would never get certified. She simply said, "You will know to stop when you can't not do it anymore." It was a new perspective to consider. I didn't see an end in sight to complete the needed classes, yet I couldn't pull myself away because I loved it.

Her voice pushed me forward toward my purpose. So, look for those who do the same for you. Find the people who see your purpose and believe in you to carry it out.

5. Look for purpose in your pain.

I discussed pain early on, but it is important to consider it again here. The pain and experiences of your past may have uniquely qualified you for your purpose today.

This one is hard, I know, but the reality is pain will be a piece of your story. So, why waste it? Pain can be a platform for God to reveal a purpose in your life. Once you have lived through it, you are best positioned to help someone else live through it, too. And doing that may give you a sense of purpose you never thought possible.

I used to coach a man named Scott Rigsby, a speaker who lives on purpose and makes an impact around the world. Scott was in a tragic accident when he was eighteen years old and lost both of his legs. He was also the first double amputee to complete the Kona Ironman. Basically, he is amazing!

As his coach, I listened to him field questions at a corporate event. I was struck by one question someone from the audience asked: "If given the chance, would you get your legs back?" Without hesitation, Scott responded, "Absolutely not! Because I would lose my purpose."

Because of the purpose he found in his own hardship, Scott has helped so many people through their pain. He works closely with veterans who have lost limbs and has done incredible things to inspire the amputee community. Now, when I struggle to see purpose in my seasons of pain, I think about Scott. I pray that, like him, my painful experiences can have purpose. That they may become someone else's survival guide.

So, as you consider your purpose, ask yourself: Is there some purpose I can find in my pain?

And remember, there are so many unique pieces of you that God can use to carry out your purpose. So many pieces of your life can assist you with your assignment. Who you are is needed in your family, community, and the world. I pray that you will invite Him into your calling and let Him push you toward a life on purpose.

Who You Are

- When in your life have you felt as though you were operating on purpose?
- Think through your strengths, past experiences, and phases of life. What do those things show about your purpose?

- Does your purpose change in different seasons of your life?
- How does the world benefit when you live out your purpose?

Whose You Are

- Is it possible that God has you here for an assignment?
- How could God confirm for you when you are living out your purpose?
- In the body of Christ, how might your purpose matter?

A Prayer

Dear God,

Thank You for using someone like me to carry out Your purpose. Lord, I know my ultimate purpose is to know You and make You known. Clarify the details for me. I want to be focused on what is important to You. Would You show me how You want me to live on purpose? Would You point me to people and places that can benefit from the gifts You have given me? Help me to stay focused on the purpose You have just for me. Use me to carry out a purpose that is larger than myself.

Help me look through the lens of Your love and trust that You worked out all the details in my life to point me to Your purpose. I pray You are shaping who I am. Mold me into who You want me to be and help me reflect Your love to the world.

Take all my pieces and use them to point others to You.

Amen.

A Truth to Remember

For we are God's handiwork, created in Christ Jesus to do good works, which God prepared in advance for us to do (Ephesians 2:10 NIV).

CHAPTER NINE
The Next Piece

It was spring break in Amelia Island. We'd met two of our best couple friends for a beach camping trip. We had never camped with the kids before and honestly weren't sure what to expect.

Day one, pretty seamless.
Day two, pretty perfect.
Day three, things changed.

After a great day on the beach, we heard rumblings from other campers about storms coming in as we made our way in for lunch. We brushed it off, assuming it would be another pop-up beach shower that passed through quickly. But as soon as the alerts for severe storms started buzzing on our phones, we realized we were wrong.

I'll stop right here and tell you what we learned: When you are in a tent and large campers start pulling out, you should follow them.

We didn't.

Instead, we all came up with very different ideas about what we should do.

Let's hunker down at camp. I think we'll be fine.
We could head to dinner and let the storms pass.
Maybe we should head to the bathhouse to take shelter in case it gets really bad.
Let's pack up what we need for the night and drive to the nearest hotel.
I say we shove everything in the car and drive all night to get home.

Without a clear plan, we were scrambling. With just fifteen minutes to spare before the storm arrived, things weren't looking good. I was throwing all our belongings in the car without any rhyme or reason. Kip was on the phone looking for a hotel nearby. Some of our kids were blissfully playing while others cried that the trip was cut short. One friend was tying down the tarps to keep their tent secure, while another was tearing down their tent altogether.

It was a cluster of storms and a cluster of a situation. We were in a panic, and each of us had a different idea about what to do next. We never collaborated or stopped to tell each other what we were doing. So, as the eye of the storm passed over us, we created our own disaster trying to figure it out. Collectively, we had no vision. We had a goal—keep the kids safe—but we had no clear plan for how to do that. We were trying to carry it out in entirely different ways, each one crippling the outcome of the other.

To move forward firmly in your identity, you must plan your future intentionally. Your future takes who you have become through past pain, relationships, and experiences, and it helps you walk forward. It gives you vision. And this is a big deal because vision is a massive piece of who you are. Like most things, I hope it's informed by Whose you are.

Creating a vision allows you to focus on the future and start seeing yourself where you want to be. It requires you to look forward and say, "Who do I want to be? What does God have for me?" That's your vision; getting to it will require you to put some faith in action.

I have a friend who owns and operates a Chick-fil-A franchise. Over the years, he has helped some of the students we serve through Lydia's Place by hiring them. During the interview process, he asks his applicants about plans for their future, and they often have no idea what they want to do with their lives. Through those interviews, one thing has become clear: So many of the kids we work with cannot describe a vision for their lives. When students get to us, they are typically in survival mode and can't even think about next week, let alone their long-term future. It's hard to name a vision when you haven't seen a model for what it could be.

Young adults aren't the only ones who struggle with this. I've spent years teaching people about creating a vision specifically for their careers. Here is the problem I've encountered time and again in this lesson: Most people have arrived at their current place in life haphazardly. They didn't have a vision for it.

As a coach, I have often asked, "How did you get here?" The answer I'm usually met with goes something like this: "Well, I got out of school, and I needed a job. I knew someone in this company, so they hired me. I worked there, then I moved to the next thing, got married, had kids, and this is it."

Sometimes, I push back with another question, "Okay, but do you like it? Do you like where your life and career have led you?" I can't tell you how often I've heard, "Oh no, I hate my job, but I only have ten years left. It's not what I thought I'd be doing or where my life would be, but it's fine."

I believe the body of Christ can do better than this type of "fine." So, I want to know what more than fine looks like for you. What do you desire for your life? Who do you want to be, and where do you want God to lead you? The answer is your vision coming to life.

Of course, actually naming that vision is tricky, especially for women. Because women tend to craft a vision for their lives around other people's needs. And while there's certainly nothing wrong with considering loved ones, women must be careful not to forsake their vision for others.

So often, I find myself sitting in the stands, cheering on everyone else. The struggle is real! It is hard to have vision when I am changing diapers, trying to recall which breast I fed from last, and generally just managing a household of people who all need something from me at the same time all the time. When my only vision is bedtime, it can be hard to see past the day ahead.

Currently, my afternoons are filled with dance classes and horseback riding lessons. My phone is filled with videos and photos of my children so that every family member gets the attention they deserve. My energy is often geared toward cheering on Kip and his career as he supports our family. In any spare time I find, I pour energy into Lydia's Place to ensure our students get what they need. And at the end of all that, it's easy to feel like all I've done is sit in the stands and root for everyone else.

This may look a little different for you. Maybe you're carrying so much extra workload at your job that you have little time to give to anything else. Your relationships may require a lot of attention and effort, leaving you emotionally spent. Maybe you're caring for a loved one or family member, and that has become your sole focus. No matter what it is, it's easy to lose sight of your vision because you're so busy worrying about everyone else.

Again, while this may be a season, it isn't forever. And even in this season, I'm learning to step back and ask God, "What's your vision for me now?" I truly believe that God is sitting in the stands of my life, watching me and rooting me on. I believe He is for me, and He wants good for me. And I believe He will lead me in the vision He has for me in any season.

Most people have a vision for what they want in their future. They may envision world travel, financial security, or influence. But when those dreams aren't rooted in the vision God has given us for our lives, they'll always come up feeling hollow.

So, you must be open to not just God's leading in giving you a vision for your life but also His leading as that vision may change. Dear friend, let me ask you this question: Has this ever been the case for you? Have you ever had a clear vision for your life that didn't come to fruition?

Your vision may have been watching kids grow up, but now you are staring at a cancer diagnosis. The boss that needs to leave for you to move up will never retire. The person you wanted to marry chose someone else. You weren't selected for the perfect job. The friendship is over. The dream house you were considering just sold. Maybe the marriage ended, your parent passed, or there is a conversation you will never get to have. That dream vacation you planned was an absolute disaster. Your child will not get into the college you hoped for, the adoption didn't go through, or the grandkids you always wanted aren't going to be. Maybe you feel like your life looks like a cluster, and there is no clear way to fix it.

Any of it can happen.
Dreams get dashed.
Plans crash and burn.

I get it. I can tell you what wasn't in my picture-perfect plan: a blended family with four girls and a twenty-year age gap in the middle of them. It wasn't the vision I had for my life at all. My vision of family had to shift. But can I tell you something else? I would've missed out on more contentment than I could've imagined if I had not been open to a new dream—God's plan for my life.

Friend, I don't want you to miss that for yourself! If the vision you always hoped for is gone, grieve what you've lost. But then, make room for a fork in the road. Because trust me, God has a new vision waiting just around the bend.

I've seen this time and again in my life, particularly with my family. After seven years of marriage, Kip and I knew it was time to make a change for our growing family. A new house with more land—that was the vision. My dad encouraged us to think specifically about what we wanted and be patient until we could get it. He was helping us craft a vision for our home, and by pursuing that in faith, we ended up with something bigger than we had even dared to imagine for ourselves.

But our vision was for more than the house itself. It was about the family we hoped to build inside of it. So, on the day we closed on our home, we walked the perimeter of our yard and prayed together.

We prayed that this would be a house of welcome. We prayed that we would make people feel comfortable and included here. We prayed for God to expand our family.

That was our vision.

We closed on our house in March. In April, Maria reached out to me from Nigeria. I had met Maria just once in Orlando at a camp where I spoke. Four years later, she had been offered the chance to become a camp counselor at the same camp. This time, the camp was in Atlanta, close to home for me, and I would be speaking there again.

So, I kept in touch with Maria over the next few months, asking her for pictures of where she lived and learning more about her story. Kip and I agreed that Maria could stay with us for two weeks while I took her to look at colleges. After only three days of having Maria in our home, Kip sat on the couch and said, "An angel has landed in our house. She can stay forever. Just go figure out how."

All those years that my heart broke waiting on a baby, all the prayers I prayed with my fists drawn at God for not completing our family, all the tears I'd cried—it all pointed to this moment. God gave us a vision to fill our home with children, and then He provided that child who needed a home right there in our living room.

I think our Heavenly Father does this all the time. He has bigger plans than I can even fathom. I believe He is most honored when I invite Him into my big visions—the things I could never do on our my own. I've learned along the way that developing a vision for my life comes from one place: reliance on Whose I am. When I'm following God, I can trust the vision He's given me. Why? Because He knows every piece of who I am.

So, how do you get there? If vision drives you to who you hope to become and the life God calls you to live, then how do you start?

1. Pray for clarity.

Discovering your vision takes time. I certainly believe God will prompt and guide you, but pray and listen first. You have to be very careful when you name your vision and call it God's. You've probably heard people say things like, "The Lord told me to ..." when talking about their vision. Could this be true? Absolutely! But I would caution you to use those words wisely. It's easy to name what you want to do and slap God's blessing on it so you can march forward. Then, you're not marching toward God's vision; you're marching toward your own.

How do you know the difference? For me, the answer lies in prayer. So, pray first. Ask God to clarify your vision. Pray for His peace and wisdom to lead you. And then, keep praying for clarity.

Listen, I want to do a lot of things. I have so many plans and dreams that it can be hard to focus. But without clarifying the vision, I run the risk of wandering aimlessly down a path I didn't intend. And friend, so do you! So, start by praying for clarity about where God is calling you.

Start with just one area in your life to craft a vision for. Write down several big categories—work, family, finances, character, faith, and relationships. Then, ask God to help you focus on a vision for just one and trust Him to carry it out.

2. Risk being uncomfortable.

Most people have a specific tendency when it comes to change or trying something new.

Some people sit very still. They wait for all the details and information or perfect circumstances before moving forward. Sometimes, they even call this "waiting on God." Other people tend to jump in and get started without enough time to pray and pause for God's direction.

In both, there is risk, but I would argue the biggest risk of all is missing the discomfort. Sometimes, waiting is used as an excuse to stay in what's comfortable. And sometimes, people jump in because they want to be in control of the plan. Both are ultimately trying to stay in the comfort zone, a place I'd argue real vision can't exist. So, whatever your tendency, work hard to become comfortable with the opposite. Adjust your first reaction. Be ready to risk getting uncomfortable.

You might have guessed by now that I'm more of a jump-right-in type of person. I like to think I can figure things out on my own, and that's typically the attitude I take toward any vision I have for my life. Maria, on the other hand, is more of a wait-and-pray type of person. So, as we've worked together to pursue her vision of graduating college, we've had to meet each other in the middle. I have had to encourage her to meet deadlines, while she has had to push me to wait and make sure she is intentional about what is next for her. We've each had to step into our discomfort to see the vision come to life.

And that risk has been worth the reward.

3. Get started.

Let's be honest. Admitting the vision you have for your future can be exciting, but it can also be scary. It opens you up to all kinds of vulnerabilities along the way.

What if I'm wrong?
What if I fail?
What if people think it's a silly dream?
What if God isn't actually leading me this way?

I could go on and on down this rabbit hole! But let me just remind you: God is for you, God is with you, and God is leading you. Because of that alone, you can push past your fear in pursuit of His vision for your life.

Start by naming your fear. Give that to God! Tell Him what you're afraid of. Ask Him to show you the way even when you're unsure. I think you'll be surprised at just how quickly God moves your fear into faith!

My friend Cissy is a great example of this. She invited me to a meal with some other ladies so I could share my vision for Lydia's Place. As I spoke about all the work we'd done so far, she cut in and asked, "What's your next goal?"

At this, I paused. "Well, I think next year I'd like to do a basket drive to collect items for our students when they arrive in their dorms."

She asked me why I was waiting until next year. I responded, "There's no way I could get it done this year; the students move in next month."

Cissy shook her head vigorously in reply. "That is not the God I know. He doesn't want to hear about what we can't do; He is interested in what we can do with Him."

With one simple sentence, she encouraged me to push past the fear of failing. God showed up. He didn't just double my projected collection; He tripled it. Had I let my fear keep me from starting, I would've missed seeing this vision come to life in far greater ways than I expected.

Remember, indecision is a decision. Even if you don't know the outcome and even if you don't have it all worked out, just start. You can't wait for perfect circumstances or all the information to get started. You can simply decide to trust God with this piece of your life and faithfully jump in.

4. Write it down.

When I was fourteen, my dad walked through the garage door wearing a fancy suit. He was crying and carrying a dozen red roses. All of this got my attention because my dad rarely dressed that nicely, and while he did bring my mom flowers frequently, I had only seen him cry once before that day. I had no idea this had been an important day. He gave my mom the roses alongside a check that came from the sale of his company. Then he gave Richard and I both a pack of index cards. (Good thing we didn't know his company was for sale, or we might have wished for more than index cards!)

Unbeknownst to us, my dad had a vision to one day sell his company. The vision was so clear that he wrote the amount he wanted to make when he sold it on an index card. He carried that card around for more than a decade. Every time he put his hand in his pocket, the index card would remind him of his vision. That day, he presented Mom with a check for an amount that exceeded what was written on the card. My dad never lost sight of his vision, and God blew it out of the water. So, he wanted to instill in my brother and me the chance to see the same thing come to fruition.

He wanted us to write down our vision with faith and confidence.

And that's exactly what I want you to do, too! Pray first. Then, get that index card and put words to the vision blooming in your heart. Pray over it, name it, and believe God will lead you to it. Where is God moving you now? Write down the answer He puts on your heart, and let it be a roadmap to see His faithfulness play out along the way.

I have no idea what your vision might be, but I know God does. And I know when you pursue that vision, you will find confidence knowing it's rooted in the truth of Whose you are. The One who designed the pieces of who you are is the same One who will lead you where He wants your life to go.

Who You Are

- As you consider your vision for your life, is it overwhelming or exciting? Why?
- Do you already have a vision? Or do you need to continue praying about and exploring this?
- What do you feel prompted or convicted about as a possible vision?
- How might you commit to exploring and taking steps toward your vision in the coming weeks?

- What is your main concern that holds you back from committing to your vision?

Whose You Are

- Can you describe a time when your past experience with God gave you the courage to try something beyond your capacity?
- Would it change your vision if you trusted that God is on your side? Would it give you the boldness to try something different?
- How has knowing Whose you are informed the vision you have for your life right now?
- Have you prayed about your vision and invited God in?
- What will you write on your index card? How can you lift that up to God to invite Him to lead you toward that vision?

A Prayer

Dear God,

Please show me clearly what You want me to do and where You want me to focus. Help me move past the vision I had for my life into the one that You have for me. Clarify my vision and help me see what You have planned for me. Help me not miss the vision that You have for me by wishing I had a different one. When it feels like I have lost my way, find me and guide me. I want to please You, God, so give me a vision pleasing to You.

Help me look through the lens of Your love and trust that You worked out all the details in my life to give me a vision that is from You. I pray You are shaping who I am. Mold me into who You want me to be and help me reflect Your love to the world.

Take all my pieces and use them to point others to You.

Amen.

A Truth to Remember

Now all glory to God, who is able, through his mighty power at work within us, to accomplish infinitely more than we might ask or think (Ephesians 3:20 NLT).

Conclusion

My grandmother collected puzzles.

I can't remember a time when I walked into Gram's house when there wasn't a puzzle on the table in various stages of completion. Anyone who walked by could stop to admire it or add a few pieces. Gram worked on countless puzzles in her lifetime. In her later years, she had one framed for each of her children and grandchildren. Occasionally, Gram would get to the final few pieces of the puzzle and realize one piece was missing. It didn't bother her; if a piece was missing, she just enjoyed the pieces that were present. Once, she had just finished a 500-piece puzzle, but it slid off the table and onto the floor. She just laughed and said, "We will do it again tomorrow." Yes, she enjoyed both the process and the outcome.

I think there is a part of us that craves for our lives to be packaged a bit like a puzzle. That way, all the pieces make sense and fit together in a nice, wrapped package. Sure, it sounds good in theory, but in reality, the picture-perfect puzzle-piece life isn't all it's cracked up to be. While puzzles are fun to work on and pretty to look at, they are also flat. They are one-dimensional. With a puzzle, there is only one picture, one outcome, one way to make the pieces fit.

I believe there is something better.

I heard a quote by Erin Hanson that struck me:

Her soul is like a kaleidoscope, busting with every shade and hue. But shift your gaze ever so slightly and she's something entirely new.[6]

Isn't this what's so great about a kaleidoscope? It's made up of so many different pieces.

Pieces that never really find their permanent place.
Pieces that don't seem to fit or make sense at all.
Pieces that come together to create beautiful patterns.
Pieces that change when you change the way you look at them.
Pieces designed to reflect light and beauty to the world.

Like a kaleidoscope, your random pieces can be beautiful as they take shape. Every piece of who you are can be used for good by Whose you are.

The pieces you compare …
The pieces passed down to you from the generation before you …
The pieces that bring pain …
The pieces that connect you to others …
The pieces that build your beliefs …
The pieces that give you rules and boundaries …
The pieces that show what you value …
The pieces that give you purpose …
The pieces that show you the vision for what's ahead.

None of it is by accident. None of it is wasted. All of it—every piece of who you are—is part of the plan for your life created by Whose

---

6   Hanson, @thepoeticunderground. Poem by Erin Hanson. *Instagram*, 25 Jan. 2016, https://www.instagram.com/p/BA9JoriBHzH/

you are, the Divine artist who never wastes a piece. Instead, God paints it all into an unfolding canvas. Every random piece of who you are can be used for the good of Whose you are. When you allow God to hold your pieces in His Hands, He can make turns and twists into beauty that continues to grow and evolve with each new relationship and experience.

The only way you can embrace this fully is to take all your pieces and place them in the hands of your Father. There, they can become whole. There, they can be used to reflect His goodness, His mercy, His love, and His light back to a world that desperately needs to see it.

You are at your best—your brightest—when you angle your lives toward the light of your Father. Then, like in a kaleidoscope, you can see a reflection of His love through your scattered pieces.

My friend, may you continue to allow God to move and twist every piece of who you are so that you can best reflect Whose you are.

Acknowledgements

A special thanks to my Kaleidoscopes, Amy, Cissy, Leslie, Rachel, Erin, Adrienne, Danielle, Kara, Kathryn, Laurel, Meg, Norma, Mary Ann, Maria, Lynn, Jennifer, Rikki, Katrina, Pepper, Laurie, Ashley, Kim, Angela, Rebecca, Anna, Heather, Kipper, Katelynn, Kristi, and Jules. You didn't just believe in me, you walked with me. Your stories shaped me, and I will forever be better for the pieces that you shared.

Natasha Ganem, Kay Keller, and Laura Whitaker, you went one step further and labored over these pages with me. Thank you.

Suzanne Chambers, you shared so many pieces of wisdom with me as you taught me to study God's Word. My prayer is that your teachings will gleam through these pages to make the same difference to others that they have made to me.

Yorkshire Publishing, Kent and Laura Denmark, you took a risk on me and helped push me forward. Penny Lange, you polished the pages with your attention to detail. Serena Hanson, you pulled all the pieces together to push this book forward.

Sara Shelton, in these pages you helped make the pieces of my story make sense. I am absolutely certain this book would not have come to fruition without you!

Kip, Maria, Lauren, Lydia, and Anne Marie, you are my light. Your belief in me makes me keep trying new things. Thank you for sharing our time together so that I could write.

And to my main Kaleidoscope, my mom, who has helped me pick up the pieces and pushed me forward my entire life. I am my best with you in my corner.

About the Author

April Farlow has spent 20 years motivating audiences to get out of their comfort zone, speak up and represent their values. As a corporate trainer, April has taught over 30,000 individuals and honed her skills to motivate hard to reach audiences.

April delivers! On topics such as vision development, self-confidence, communication, presentation skills, and leadership, she has led to measurable behavioral change impacting the bottom line in multiple industries.

Organizations who have heard from April include UPS (United Parcel Service), CDC (Centers for Disease Control), United States Air Force, Federal Home Loan Bank Atlanta, Home Depot, Kroger Company, Microsoft, Chick-Fil-A, Wal-Mart, Bank South, and Spanx.

While speaking at a conference for foster youth in 2009, April was moved by the students in the audience. As a result, she founded Lydia's Place, a non-profit serving young adults who have experienced foster care or homelessness. Since its start in 2017, Lydia's Place has served over 1,000 students on more than 20 college campuses around the state of Georgia. A cornerstone of Lydia's Place is to provide housing and, through partnerships with local non-profits, the organization has opened 20 bedrooms to care for young adults in need on an on-going basis.

Today, April is an advocate for the voice of young people in their transition to independence. She lives in Athens, Georgia on a mini-farm with her husband and four girls.

Visit her at aprilfarlow.com